THE SHORTER CATECHISM

Volume 2: Questions 39–107

G. I. Williamson

ILLUSTRATED BY

THOMAS TYSON

PRESBYTERIAN AND REFORMED PUBLISHING CO.
Phillipsburg, New Jersey

ISBN: 0-87552-540-7

Library of Congress Catalog Card No. 77-139855
Printed in the United States of America

To Sandra, Nancy and Cathy

LESSON ONE

Question 39. What is the duty which God requireth of man?

Answer: The duty which God requireth of man, is obedience to his revealed will.[1]

Question 40. What did God at first reveal to man for the rule of his obedience?

Answer: The rule which God at first revealed to man for his obedience, was the moral law.[2]

Question 41. Where is the moral law summarily comprehended?

Answer: The moral law is summarily comprehended in the ten commandments.[3]

Question 42. What is the sum of the ten commandments?

Answer: The sum of the ten commandments is, To love the Lord our God with all our heart, with all our soul, with all our strength, and with all our mind; and our neighbour as ourselves.[4]

1. He hath showed thee, O man, what is good; and what doth the Lord require of thee, but to do justly . . . (Micah 6:8).
2. For when the Gentiles, which have not the law, do by nature the things contained in the law, these, having not the law, are a law unto themselves. Which shew the work of the law written in their hearts . . . (Rom. 2:14,15).
3. And he gave unto Moses . . . two tables of testimony, tables of stone, written with the finger of God (Ex. 31:18).
4. See Matthew 22:37-40.

We come now to the second great section of the Catechism. Having considered (in Volume I) "what man is to believe concerning God," we now consider "what duty God requires of man." But we do well to remember that these two things can never be separated in the life of the Christian. There is no true faith without obedience. And there is no real obedience without faith. Without faith it is impossible to please God (Heb. 11:6). And faith without obedience is dead (James 2:22).

It is man's duty to obey God. The reason for this is that God is the

1

creator and man is a mere creature. Because God created man He therefore has "a right" to require what He will from man. Because man is only a creature, he has "no right" to "go his own way, and do his own will." No, the only "right" for man is to obey God. So, in the very nature of the case, the will of God is the rule by which man ought to live. And according to the Catechism this will of God for man was first revealed to man in *the moral law.* Then the Catechism goes on to say that we have this moral law "summarily comprehended" in the ten commandments, with these ten commandments themselves being summed up in the two great commandments of love (Q. 42 and Matt. 22:37-40). Now let us try to get this teaching clearly within our view. God's revealed will *is* the moral law. The moral law is (another name for) the ten commmandments. And the ten commandments are (the same thing as) the two commandements of Christ. So, just as $1 + 1 + 1 + 1 + 1 + 1 + 1 + 1 + 1 + 1 = 10$, while $5 + 5 = 10$ also; likewise, the moral law (which God gave to Adam) = the ten commandments, while the two great commandments of Christ also = the ten commandments. Or in other words: the moral law which Adam had as the rule of his obedience at the beginning of the world was essentially the same as the ten commandments that we now have in the Bible, and essentially the same as the two great commandments of love. This does not mean that Adam received the moral law in the same *form*—or in the same words—that we have in the ten commandments, or the two commandments of love. But it does mean that the sense—or meaning—was the same.

We could perhaps illustrate this by thinking of light. As we see in the illustration on the next page, light can be seen by us in two different forms. We can see it in its undivided unity. And then we can see it "broken down," as it were, into the various colors of the spectrum. And yet, the fact is that it is *the same light* that we see. It is only that we see it in two different ways. And it is exactly so with the moral law of God. God is light. His will is holy and unchangeable. Thus we can be sure that the rule which God gave Adam is essentially the same as the ten commandments, and the two commandments of love. We have proof of this, too, in the teaching of Paul (Rom. 2:14,15). (1) The Gentiles do not have "the law." They do not have the Bible, or the ten commandments in written form. (2) They do things contained in the law. This does not mean that they live holy lives. It only means that they do try to do things required in the ten commandments. (3) They are, therefore, a law unto themselves. This means that they have a moral consciousness within themselves which confronts them with the de-

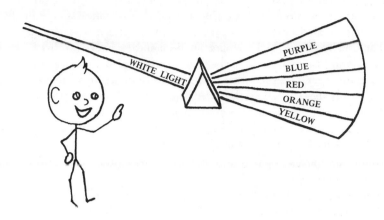

mands of the law. This can be seen in the fact that they have a conscience which either accuses or excuses them whenever they do not live up to this law. (4) So we come to Paul's verdict, which is that they have "the work of the law written in their hearts." Notice, he doesn't say that they have "the *words* of the law written in their hearts." But they do have "the *works* of the law written" there. So the form is different, but the substance is the same. And we thus see, from the Scripture itself, that the same will of God that we now have in the ten commandments, Adam originally had in his own moral consciousness or conscience. All men inherit this from him.

The question naturally arises: why did God *again* reveal the moral law if it was already written in the heart of man from the beginning? The answer to this question is simple: because of sin. Sinful men have tried very hard to get rid of their own inner sense of God's moral law. Paul says that men have tried to suppress the truth of God. "They did not like to retain God in their knowledge," he says (Rom. 1:28). "They changed the truth of God into a lie" (Rom. 1:25). And "their foolish heart was darkened" (Rom. 1:21). "Men loved darkness rather than light, because their deeds were evil" (John 3:19). But they did not succeed. Try as they would, they could not

3

entirely rid themselves of the light. They still had the work of the law written in their hearts. They still had a conscience that testified against their evil deeds. They were therefore without excuse (Rom. 1:20). Yet so far did they succeed that it was necessary for God to reveal His moral law again in the ten commandments. For only in this way could sinful men again adequately see what God required. After doing all he could to bury—or twist—or forget—the moral law of God as it spoke to him out of his own heart and conscience, it was very necessary that God speak to him *again* to reveal His holy will. For "by the law is the knowledge of sin" (Rom. 3:20). It is "our schoolmaster to bring us unto Christ, that we might be justified by faith" (Gal. 3:24). People sometimes imagine that the ten commandments were given only to the people of Israel. It is also thought by some that these ten commandments were given so that the children of Israel might earn their salvation by keeping them. The Bible clearly teaches us that this is not true. The law was given "because of transgressions" (Gal. 3:19). It was given, in other words, so that all of God's people (in both Old and New Testament times) would come to see how sinful they really are. It was given just as much for us today as for the people of God in Old Testament times. Paul does not say "by the law *was*" but "by the law *is* the knowledge of sin" (Rom. 3:20).

But if this be true—if we need the law to bring us to Christ—then why does the Catechism discuss the law *after* it tells us about the person and work of Christ? (1) The first reason is that Christ is more important than the law. If the Catechism discussed the law first, it might suggest the thought that we can be saved by the law. But it is Christ who saves us, and not the works of the law. Since He alone saves us, He must have the pre-eminence. (2) The second reason is that we are not to forget the law after Jesus has saved us. Some people have taught this. They say that a Christian is not obligated to keep the ten commandments. But all of the great catechisms of the Reformation discuss the law after they discuss the work of Christ, so that this error will be avoided. For the believer is "not without law to God, but under the law to Christ" (I Cor. 9:21). The law drives us to Christ in order to be saved. But Christ brings us back to the law because we are saved. "He that hath my commandments, and keepeth them, he it is that loveth me" (John 14:21).

A final word is in order. There are other laws in the Bible besides what we call the moral law. There are the *ceremonial* laws, having to do with the sacrificial worship of the tabernacle and temple. There are the *civil* laws also,

4

which God gave to Israel as a nation. These laws have been cancelled by the passing away of the state of affairs in which they could be applied. But it is not so with the moral law of God, contained in the ten commandments and in the two commandments of love. Jesus said that He did not come to cancel this law, but rather than fulfill it (Matt. 5:17). And the very purpose for which He saved us was that we too might turn from our sin, to begin to walk in the way of His commandments. For "by this we know that we love the children of God," says John, "when we love God, and keep his commandments. For this is the love of God, that we keep his commandments" (I John 5:2,3).

Questions:

1. What are the two subjects dealt with in the Shorter Catechism? What is the relationship between them?
2. Why does man have a duty towards God?
3. Did Adam receive the ten commandments at the beginning of history? Explain.
4. What does the illustration show us with respect to the moral law of God?
5. What does Romans 2:14,15 prove?
6. If all men already have a consciousness of moral law, why did God again reveal the moral law (in the ten commandments)?
7. Why is it wrong to say that the ten commandments were given only for the Jews?
8. What is the most important lesson that we are to learn from this schoolmaster?
9. If we need the law *first* in order to come to Christ, then why does the Catechism reverse this order?
10. What other kinds of laws are there in the Bible besides the moral law?
11. Are these other kinds of laws still in effect? Why?
12. How do we know that the moral law(s) have never been cancelled?

5

Question 42. What is the sum of the ten commandments?

Answer: The sum of the ten commandments is, to love the Lord our God with all our heart, with all our soul, with all our strength, and with all our mind; and our neighbor as ourselves.[1]

Question 43. What is the preface to the ten commandments?

Answer: The preface to the ten commandments is in these words, I am the Lord thy God, which have brought thee out of the land of Egypt, out of the house of bondage.[2]

Question 44. What doth the preface to the ten commandments teach us?

Answer: The preface to the ten commandments teacheth us, that because God is the Lord, and our God, and Redeemer, therefore we are bound to keep all his commandments.[3]

1. Matthew 22:37-40.
2. Exodus 20:2.
3. Therefore will we also serve the Lord; for he is our God (Josh. 24:18).
4. Ye are bought with a price: therefore glorify God in your body, and in your spirit, which are God's (I Cor. 6:20).

In this part of the Catechism we find two very important principles. (1) There is first the great truth that love is the fulfilling of the law. (2) Then there is the truth that when a person is saved by God this fact only increases his obligation to keep the commandments of God. Since both these principles are often denied today, we will discuss them in contrast to certain false teachings that are current.

One of these false teachings that is very popular is the notion that there is a basic conflict between law and love. The law requires one thing, it is said, but love may very well dictate another. For example, the law says that we must not lie or steal. But there may be situations, it is said, in which love for other human beings may require me to lie (to protect them) or to steal (to feed them). This concept has been called by different names ("The New Morality," "Situation Ethics," etc.). But the basic point is that, according to this teaching, love may be against law, and law may be against love. And it is the very opposite teaching that we find in the Catechism. More important by far: it is the opposite teaching that we find in the Bible, which is the inerrant word of God. Advocates of this false teaching sometimes attempt to show that Jesus went against the law in the name of love. But this is not what the Bible tells us. In the Sermon on the Mount Jesus clearly teaches us that He did not come to destroy, or abrogate, the law (Matt. 5:17). He warned His disciples against breaking any of the commandments, or teaching men to do so (Matt. 5:19). And He went on to discuss several of the commandments. He did refuse to be bound by some traditional interpretations of the law—and additions to it—which the Jews had made. But He also showed how absolute the law itself really is. He showed how it requires nothing less than perfection (Matt. 5:48). And far from saying that there is some conflict between law and love, Jesus taught His disciples that love (and love alone) leads to the keeping of the law! "If ye love me," said Jesus, "keep my commandments" (John 14:15). "He that hath my commandments, and keepeth them," He said, "he it is that loveth me" (John 14:21). "For this is the love of God, that we keep his commandments," says the inspired Apostle John (I John 5:3).

The teaching of the Catechism is confirmed by the perfect life lived by our Lord. For no one ever exemplified love—perfect love—as did He. He loved God as we ourselves ought to love God. And He loved His neighbor even as himself. But did this impel our Lord to break any of the commandments? No, it did not. For the Bible says He was "tempted like as we are" in all points, and yet was "without sin" (Heb. 4:15). And "sin is transgression of the law" (I John 3:4). We must conclude, therefore, that there is a wrong concept of love whenever there is this tendency to oppose the law of God. If we love *ourselves* with all our heart, and soul, and mind, and strength, it will not be surprising that we will feel led to do things that God forbids. This may even be the case if we love another human person (or persons) supremely. But if we love God supremely, and then our neighbor (that is, other persons) as ourselves, it will be our desire to do the will of God. We will say, "not my will, but thy will be done." And thus, love will lead to the keeping of the law.

Another false teaching that is current today is that which fails to see the unity of Old and New Testaments. The basic error in this teaching is the thought that the law of God (the ten commandments) is regarded differently in the two testaments. One form of this error is to say that the people of God in the Old Testament period were required to keep the law of God first,

7

and then were saved by God as a reward for their obedience. But we notice from the words of the preface (Q. 43, Ex. 20:2) that this is not true. When God delivered His people out of slavery in Egypt, it was not because they had kept the ten commandments. No, He first delivered them, and then gave them the ten commandments. So they were not expected to try to keep the law in order to be saved. Rather were they expected to do this *because they already had been saved*. And this is exactly the way it is in the life of the Christian. The New Testament does not say that we are to first try to keep the law of God and that then we will be saved. No, it teaches us that we must be saved first and then strive to keep God's commandments. So there is no difference at all, in this matter, between the Old and New Testaments. Another form of this same error, however, is perhaps even more pernicious. It is the thought that because Christ has kept the law of God for His people, the Christian believer does not need to keep the ten commandments. It is the teaching, in other words, that the New Testament believer has less need than the Old Testament believer to keep the ten commandments after being saved. The Bible says, "ye are bought with a price, therefore glorify God in your body, and in your spirit, which are God's" (I Cor. 6:20). One of the great principles of the Bible is that God requires more from those to whom He has given more, and less from those to whom He has given less (Luke 12:48). It was for this reason that the Israelites had a greater obligation to keep the ten commandments than did the heathen nations. But for the same reason the Christian (who has received the full benefit of the finished work of Christ) has even more reason to keep the ten commandments than did the Israelite of old.

In the next several lessons we will be considering each of these ten commandments in order. But in the remainder of this lesson we want to emphasize certain things with respect to the decalogue as a whole. (1) The first of these things is the fact that in these ten commandments we have the whole will of God expressed. We do not, for example, need new additions to this list of ten commandments. One of the things that churches need to beware is the temptation to do this. If we rightly understand the meaning of these ten commandments we will see that they are sufficient. (This truth will be more evident as we study each of these commandments.) (2) The second thing we need to observe is the fact that there is a divinely inspired order in the arrangement of these commandments. It was Jesus who said, "thou shalt worship the Lord thy God, and him only shalt thou serve" (Matt. 4:10). And it is this order that we note in the decalogue. The first four commandments teach us true worship. And the fourth commandment, in part, together with the last six teach us how we are to serve Him. Thus the two basic parts of the law manifest a divinely inspired order. And we even see this in looking more closely at each particular law. Let us illustrate this by the following diagram.

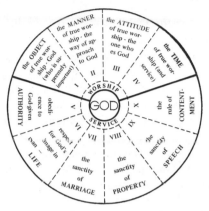

It will readily be seen that the ten commandments have an order. And it will be evident that the principle of organization is the centrality of God. God is supremely important. The more directly concerned with God a commandment is, the higher it is in the table of ten. The more indirect this concern, the lower it is. And yet, all ten commandments express duty in reference first to God, and then only to man. Sometimes Christian people have said that the first four commandments teach our duty to God, and that the last six teach our duty to man. This is not a satisfactory way of expressing it. All ten commandments teach us our duty to God primarily. It is our duty to worship God, and to serve God. And the whole of life is to be nothing more than this, by rights. This leads us to note, in conclusion, (3) that the law is an absolute unity. We cannot break one of these commandments without, in effect, breaking them all (James 2:10). Paul says that covetousness *is* idolatry (Col. 3:5). When we break the tenth commandment, in other words, we already begin to depart from the true God himself, and this is idolatry (a breaking of the first commandment).

Questions:

1. What are the two great principles taught in Catechism Questions 42-44?
2. In your own words state the two popular teachings that stand against these principles.

9

3. What did Jesus say about law and love?
4. In the life of our Lord which of these (law or love) did Christ put first? Explain.
5. What kind of love is it that leads to a disregard for, or opposition to, the ten commandments?
6. How do we know that the Old Testament people did not try to keep the law before they were saved?
7. Why can we be certain that the New Testament believer has even more reason than the Old Testament believer for keeping the law of God?
8. In your own words state the three general principles that we need to remember concerning the decalogue as a whole.
9. What "principle" is evident in the arrangement (order) of the ten commandments?
10. Why is it wrong to divide the ten commandments into "two tables"— one being our duty to God, the other our duty to man?
11. Explain why Paul can say covetousness *is* idolatry.

LESSON THREE

Question 45. Which is the first commandment?

Answer: The first commandment is, Thou shalt have no other gods before me.[1]

Question 46. What is required in the first commandment?

Answer: The first commandment requireth us to know[2] and acknowledge God to be the only true God, and our God;[3] and to worship and glorify him accordingly.[4]

1. Exodus 20:3.
2. And thou, Solomon my son, know thou the God of thy father . . . (I Chron. 28:9).
3. Thou hast avouched [declared] the Lord this day to be thy God, and to walk in his ways, and to keep his statutes, and his commandments, and his judgments, and to hearken unto his voice (Deut. 26:17).
4. Thou shalt worship the Lord thy God, and him only shalt thou serve (Matt. 4:10).

The first commandment is concerned with the *object* of true worship. The principle set forth in this commandment is this: it is the true and living God (and none other) who is to be worshiped and served by men. Before we concern ourselves about the proper manner of worship (in the second commandment), or the proper attitude (in the third commandment), or even the proper time of worship (in the fourth commandment), we must first be certain that the object of our worship is the true and living God. Here we see how contrary this commandment is to popular religious opinion. For nothing is more common than the idea that it doesn't matter what particular religion one may have, or what denomination one belongs to, since it is taken for granted by most people that those different religions have the same object in view. The different religions, in other words, are commonly thought to be just different ways of knowing one and the same God. But the Bible does not agree with this. No, it says "though there be [those] that are called gods, whether in heaven or in earth, (as there be gods many, and lords many,) but to us there is but one God, the Father, of whom are all things, and we in him; and one Lord

11

Jesus Christ, by whom are all things. and we by him" (I Cor. 8:5,6). Since there are many "gods." and since only one God is the true and living God, it becomes extremely important to know and acknowledge the true God as God.

If God were only the creation of man's imagination, then all "gods" would be "created equal." One "god" would have no higher claim than another. This is the exact truth with all the "gods" that men have made. In ancient times men created "gods" for themselves. They made these "gods" out of wood, stone, silver, gold, and so on. Today men create "gods" for themselves having no material form. They *imagine* a "god" who is without wrath, for example; a "god" who does not punish sin. Now of course these "gods" that men create in their minds have no real existence. They only *seem* real to those who "believe in them." Just as the idols in the Old Testament times were only wood or stone. so these "gods" that men have created out of their own imagination are nothing more than idols.

What the first commandment requires. then, is *that we come to know the true and living God as He really is*. This means that we must accept the teachings of the Bible. We must form our conception according to what the Scripture says, and not according to what we might wish. The Bible teaches a high view of God. It teaches us such things as the creation of the world in six days; the power of God to raise the dead from their graves; and the promise of God to make new heavens and a new earth at the end of history. It tells us that God sent Jesus Christ His only begotten Son into the world to save us from eternal punishment. It teaches us about great miracles that God has wrought. And it teaches us that there are three persons in the Godhead— the Father, Son, and Holy Ghost; and that these three are one God, the same in substance, equal in power and glory. In order to know the true and living God, then, one must certainly have some acquaintance with what the Bible teaches. For "how shall they believe in him of whom they have not heard?" (Rom. 10:14).

It is not so easy to say just *how much* of the Bible a person must know in order to know the true and living God. The thief on the cross probably did not know that Jesus was born of the virgin Mary. He may not have grasped the doctrine of the trinity in the same clearly defined way that we learn to know it in the Shorter Catechism. We can only say that he had sufficient revelation of the true and living God to know the difference between this true God and all other gods. And it is important to observe that such revelation as he did receive, and understand, he fully acknowledged or embraced. There is a world of difference, in other words. between such a man as this

12

thief and a modern-day person who knows much of what the Bible teaches but then rejects a part of it. If the thief did not believe in the "virgin birth of Christ," in other words, this was simply due to ignorance. But there are those today who know very well that the Bible teaches this doctrine, but they are not willing to believe it. This is very different. For when we do not accept God's revelation of himself in the Scripture, we do not "acknowledge God to be the only true God." And we do not "worship and glorify him accordingly."

A very common idea today concerns us here: it is the thought that one can know and acknowledge the true God without being concerned about the particular church to which one belongs. Some even go so far as to belong to no church at all, on the grounds that one may acknowledge God secretly. People had much the same view in Elijah's day. "And Elijah came unto all the people and said, how long halt ye between two opinions? if the Lord be God, follow him: but if Baal, then follow him. And the people answered him not a word." The command of God is that we confess our faith before men (Matt. 10:32), and that we separate ourselves from an unfaithful church (II Cor. 6:17) in order to belong to a faithful church of Jesus Christ (Acts 2:41-47). We do not really *acknowledge* the true God, in other words, unless we openly commit ourselves to Him, and to His cause in the world.

It would be a great mistake, however, to think of this first commandment—and of what it requires—only in terms of *church* membership and the like. For the first commandment requires us to acknowledge the true God, and to glorify Him, *in the whole of life*. God alone must be supreme, in other words, in everything! Anything less than this is, from the biblical point of view, a falling short of what is required in this commandment. Let us try to illustrate this truth by considering for a moment just one sphere of human activity, the sphere of education.

According to law there is to be no "sectarian teaching" in the public school. What this means is that teachers are not allowed to teach *what the Bible says*

THE PUBLIC SCHOOL

THE CHRISTIAN SCHOOL

13

about God, man, and the world. But the Christian point of view is that this (what the Bible says) *must* be taught in the schools that Christians send their children to, and that such (false) teachings as the theory of evolution not be taught to their children *as the truth*. It is for this reason that Christian people have organized Christian schools in order that the true and living God might be supreme in the education that their children receive. And one of the things that has stimulated this activity is the fact that the United States Supreme Court has ruled again and again against *God's* rightful place in this sphere of American public life.

There are other spheres of human endeavor that require the same sort of response from Christians today. We mention the need for labor unions and political parties that openly acknowledge the supremacy of God. But these are only other examples. What we need to realize above all is that those who really know God, and acknowledge Him, can never be satisfied with anything wherein God is ignored, or given less than that which is His due. It is this great truth—that God is supreme over all, and that all of life is religion—that distinguishes consistent Christianity from so much that is found in the world (even under the Christian name). Those who have come to see what this first commandment means will no longer think of life as a two-compartment affair—with religion in one compartment and the rest of life in the other. Neither will such a person think of religion as *merely* a matter of getting souls saved. It is that, but it is also much more than that. It is also a matter of striving to be faithful to God in business, and in recreation, and in politics, and so on.

It is here, too, that we can see what James meant when he said that we cannot break one commandment without breaking the whole law! Since God is supreme, and since our supreme duty is to know and acknowledge Him in the whole of life, the other nine commandments could be thought of as aspects of this commandment. The other nine commandments, in other words, teach us how we can worship and glorify the true God as we should. It is when we receive these commandments as the commandments of the true and living God that we honor Him. It is when we sincerely strive to keep them because we love God, and want to please Him, that we do receive them aright. For, as John said, "this is the love of God, that we keep his commandments" (I John 5:3). This enables us to see how wrong it is to take only some of the commandments rather than the decalogue as a whole. People who do not attend church services, or worship God, sometimes pride themselves on the fact that they try to keep these commandments that have to do with their relationship to other people (Commandments 5-10). But from God's point of view, we do not even begin to keep any of His commandments aright until we first recognize the supremacy of God, and *then* strive to obey these commandments in order that we might please Him!

Questions:

1. With what is the first commandment concerned? Explain what this means.
2. What is the basic principle set forth in this commandment?
3. What popular opinion is completely contradicted by this commandment?
4. Are there other "gods" besides the true and living God? Explain.
5. Do men "make idols" today? If so, how?
6. Why are all "gods" not equal?
7. How can we come to know the true and living God?
8. Is it possible to come to know the true God in ignorance of what the Bible teaches? Explain.
9. In your own words tell why two men might both lack belief in the doctrine of the virgin birth and yet one have, and one not have, saving faith.
10. Can we "acknowledge" the true God according to Scripture without public profession of faith and church membership?
11. How does the public school system in America violate this commandment?
12. What other spheres does this commandment concern?
13. How does this commandment (when properly understood) enrich our conception of the Christian life?
14. How does this commandment relate to the other nine commandments?

LESSON FOUR

Question 47. What is forbidden in the first commandment?

Answer: The first commandment forbiddeth the denying,[1] or not worshipping and glorifying the true God as God,[2] and our God;[3] and the giving of that worship and glory to any other, which is due to him alone.[4]

Question 48. What are we specially taught by these words (*before me*) in the first commandment?

Answer: These words (*before me*) in the first commandment teach us, that God, who seeth all things,[5] taketh notice of, and is much displeased with, the sin of having any other god.[6]

1. The fool hath said in his heart, there is no God (Ps. 14:1).
2. When they knew God, they glorified him not as God (Rom. 1:21).
3. But my people would not hearken to my voice: and Israel would none of me (Ps. 81:11).
4. Who changed the truth of God into a lie, and worshipped and served the creature more than the creator (Rom. 1:25).
5. All things are naked and opened unto the eyes of him with whom we have to do (Heb. 4:13).
6. They provoked him to jealousy with strange gods (Deut. 32:16).

If there is but one only, living and true God, then He alone ought to be worshiped. If this true God has made himself known to us through His inspired Word (the Bible), then we ought to be careful that we do not confuse Him with idols. Yet this is the very thing we are so often tempted to do.

Syncretism is the attempted blending of irreconcilable principles. Religious syncretism is the attempt to harmonize the true religion with the many false religions of this world. And it is *this* sin that the first commandment warns us against. We may not, under any circumstances, act as if the God of the Bible and the false gods of this world are one and the same. This, for example, is the basic evil in many secret organizations such as the *Order of Freemasons* (commonly called the Masonic Lodge). Freemasonry is, in its own words, "that natural religion in which all men agree." In other words, according to

16

the teaching of this lodge, the Christian, the Jew, the Muslim, and so on, can assemble together as a religious fellowship, and unite in prayer to the Great Architect of the Universe. This is possible, says Freemasonry, because men of all faiths worship the same deity under different forms. Thus it is said that Freemasonry "in no way conflicts with any other religion, unless that religion holds that no one outside its portals can be saved" (J. S. M. Ward, *Freemasonry: Its Aims and Ideals*, p. 187). Or, in other words, Freemasonry is the religion which says—as its most basic principle—that all "gods" are equal. But the Bible denies this very thing above all. "For there is one God, and one mediator between God and men" (I Tim. 2:5). No man can come to God except through Jesus Christ (John 14:6). "Whosoever denieth the Son, the same hath not the Father" (I John 2:23). It is for this reason that the Christian may not have religious fellowship with any person until that person professes faith in Jesus Christ (II John 10). This is the reason why no consistent Christian may become—or remain—a member of any organization such as the Order of Freemasons. He may not do this because God does not allow the Christian believer to act *as if* false religions are true, or *as if* false gods are the same as the true God. It is quite true, of course, that "there is not in every man this knowledge" (I Cor. 8:7). Sometimes we even find Christians who do not understand that they are not to engage in religious syncretism. But our duty is not to be determined by man's confused state of mind. It is to be determined by God's revelation in Scripture, and that alone.

But let us not imagine that the danger of syncretism is found in religious orders alone. No, the truth is that much of our society today is tainted with this same evil. Let us give an example. When a President is inaugurated it is the custom to ask representatives of various religions to offer prayer. A Jewish rabbi will pray, and then a Roman Catholic priest, followed by a minister of some Protestant denomination. The common notion is that no matter who is praying God will accept the prayer. And we often notice that people will bow their heads and join in the prayer, no matter who is leading. Does this not indicate that people generally assume that all are praying to the same God, no matter what their religion may be? This, again, is syncretism, and a violation of the first commandment. The rabbi does not accept the Lord Jesus as the Christ of God. He does not believe that Jesus is God. But the Bible says that this is the true God (I John 5:20). Jesus Christ is the true God and there is no other! How can a Christian be faithful to Christ, then, and pray with someone who does not acknowledge Christ? Of course the differences that separate Protestant and Catholic may not be this great. But

17

suppose the priest prays *to* the virgin Mary! Here again the consistent Christian simply cannot participate.

The democratic concept of religion is often called "non-sectarian." What it really means, in practice, is that we are urged to forget the things that divide and separate us, and unite on the basis of those things wherein we agree. On this basis some have proposed that there be "non-sectarian" prayer in the public schools. But let us clearly understand that this is at least as bad as no prayer at all. "Non-sectarian" prayer means prayer that leaves Jesus out. (Otherwise the Jews would be offended.) This is the very thing that God forbids in the first commandment. We may never leave Jesus out, and then join with others in anything religious as if we all worshiped the same God.

A third way in which we are tempted to violate this commandment is by a wrong kind of attitude of tolerance. Here we see one of Shorty's friends pointing to his church. But it is a Mormon church, and according to the teaching of the Bible the Mormons do not worship the one living and true God. It is therefore the duty of the Christian to witness (to tell about Jesus Christ, and the only way of salvation) to Mormon people. But the temptation is to remain silent. The temptation is to act as if it didn't make much difference

what religion a person happens to have. It is quite true, of course, that every person has (and ought to have) a *civil liberty* to choose whatever religion he will. No government should ever force people to accept the true religion. Christians should even be willing to defend members of a false religion if they are persecuted or coerced. But no man has a right before God—a religious right—to choose any religion but that of the Bible. In God's sight it is the duty of every man to believe in Jesus Christ, and accept the teachings of the Scriptures. And the Christian may not act as if it makes no difference in God's sight whether or not people do this. Without the use of any kind of force the Christian must let such people know that their religion is wrong, and that they will be rejected by God unless they repent and believe.

Finally, we must mention the strong temptation that comes to us today from the commonly accepted idea of *religious neutrality*. Much of what we see in modern life, in various aspects of society, is molded by the idea that it is possible to be neither for nor against any particular religion. Much of what our government is doing is ruled by this concept: it takes no stand for, or against, any particular religion. This is the theory, the idea. But Jesus said, "he that is not with me is against me" (Luke 11:23). And this means that religious neutrality is simply impossible. If we do not profess Jesus Christ as the one true God, then—by not doing so—we profess ourselves to refuse His claims. If we profess nothing, in other words, we profess much—because actions speak as loudly (at least) as words. It is for this reason that Christian people have begun to realize that those who are not for Christ are really against Him. They are beginning to realize that Christ has been denied in one sphere of life and society after another under the innocent-sounding claim of religious neutrality. That is why it is imperative that Christian people work together to rebuild on a Christian basis. We must have schools, for example, which are for Jesus Christ. But in truth, every human activity—and organized form of activity—ought to be carried out on a thoroughly Christian basis.

False religion is often willing to support a supposed neutrality. This is to be expected. The one thing that false religion needs is to neutralize true religion. If true religion can be silenced, so that it does not witness against error, then error will advance. Then, by and by, when error becomes strong enough it can use force to persecute true religion. This is what has happened again and again. It is what is happening today. Christians must awake. They must learn to see the idea of religious neutrality for what it really is—a clever deception of Satan. Let it be said once again: there can be no religious neutrality. Let it further be said that there is no area of life in which there can be religious neutrality. It matters not what sphere of life—or what kind of activity we engage in—all ought to manifest open loyalty to Jesus Christ. And this means open rejection of every other god. To Jesus belongs that name which is above every name (Phil. 2:9). To that name every knee must bow.

19

Questions:

1. What is *syncretism*?
2. How does the Order of Freemasons violate the first commandment?
3. Why may not Christians have religious fellowship with adherents of other religions?
4. How is the danger of syncretism evident in our society?
5. What does "non-sectarian" prayer mean?
6. Why is this kind of prayer wrong for the Christian?
7. In what sense ought we to be tolerant of other religions?
8. In what sense ought we to be intolerant of other religions?
9. What is meant by "religious neutrality"?
10. Is there such a thing as "religious neutrality"? Explain.
11. Why does false religion favor religious neutrality?
12. What is our responsibility today in a society that seems more and more dominated with the idea of religious neutrality?

Question 49. Which is the second commandment?

Answer:　　　The second commandment is, Thou shalt not make unto thee any graven image, or any likeness of any thing that is in heaven above, or that is in the earth beneath, or that is in the water under the earth: thou shalt not bow down thyself to them nor serve them: for I the Lord thy God am a jealous God, visiting the iniquity of the fathers upon the children unto the third and fourth generation of them that hate me, and showing mercy unto thousands of them that love me and keep my commandments.

Question 50. What is required in the second commandment?

Answer:　　　The second commandment requireth the receiving, observing,[1] and keeping pure and entire, all such religious worship and ordinances as God hath appointed in his word.[2]

1. Teaching them to observe all things whatsoever I have commanded . . . (Matt. 28:20).
2. What thing soever I command you, observe to do it: thou shalt not add thereto, nor diminish from it (Deut. 12:32).

The Roman Catholic Church and the Lutheran Churches treat the second commandment as if it were a part of the first commandment. In order to do this, and still have *ten* commandments, they divide the tenth commandment into two parts. We believe that this is a misrepresentation of the second commandment. For it is evident that we do not need two commandments forbidding the same sin (coveting). And we do need a commandment to tell us *how* to worship God. If the second commandment is not considered as a separate commandment, then we do not have any commandment to tell us that God must be worshiped according to His will!

This is the great principle contained in the second commandment: the duty *to worship God as He himself commands.* This means (as we shall see further in our next lesson) that God may not be worshiped properly in any way in-

21

vented by men. In order to bring out clearly what we mean, let us study the following diagram.

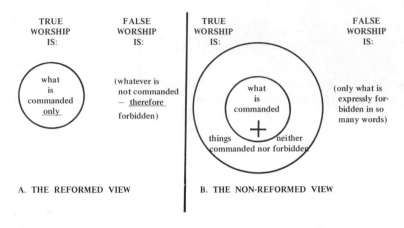

A. THE REFORMED VIEW | B. THE NON-REFORMED VIEW

It will be clear, from this diagram. that true worship (according to the Reformed view) will contain only such elements as can be proved from Scripture to be the will of God. Thus there will be the reading and preaching of the Scriptures, singing of psalms, administration of the sacraments of baptism and the Lord's Supper, and prayer. Here we see the simplicity and spiritual nature of Reformed worship. But in such a church as the Roman Catholic, or Lutheran, for example, there will be the other view (Figure B). In this view, the things commanded by God constitute only a part (often only a *small* part) of what is considered to be true worship. The Roman Church therefore has seven sacraments, only two of which are actually commanded in Scripture. The Roman Church also finds a place for special garments for clergymen, crosses, candles, statues, and so on. And there is even room to add more of these things in the future. For (according to this view) the only thing that is wrong in the worship of God is *what God has specifically forbidden* in His word. It is wrong, for example, to use an image of Baal because the Bible expressly condemns any image of Baal. But it is not wrong to use an image of the virgin Mary, according to this view, because God has not said (in so many words) that it is wrong to use an image of Mary. In answer to this, a Reformed Christian would say: "No, God has not given us a long list of every possible thing that He would forbid in His worship. If God had done that, the Bible would be so big no one could read

22

it all. What God has done is to give us a simple principle. And by this principle we know that *what He commands is sufficient*, and that *what He does not command is therefore forbidden.*"

It is quite clear, from the above diagram, that many Protestants (and even many who profess to be Presbyterian and Reformed) really hold the non-reformed view. This is plain to see from the fact that many of the things that were once excluded from these churches are being introduced anew. Thus we see in these churches too, special garments for ministers, crosses, candles, uninspired hymns, and so on. It is sad to see this because these things—being mere human inventions, and not commanded by God—are not only of no help to true worship, but are in actual fact a hindrance to it. The reason for this is that God is a spirit, and those who worship Him must worship Him in spirit and in truth (John 4:24). "The Lord of heaven and earth, dwelleth not in temples made with hands; neither is worshipped with men's hands" (Acts 17:24, 25). When men see a great cathedral, or a stained glass window—or when they hear a great choir, or a mighty organ—they are indeed moved. These things have the power to touch our emotions. But this is just as true in the case of a non-Christian as it is in the case of a Christian. Unbelievers too can feel moved by these things. And—this is the key point— none of these are of any value whatsoever in conveying the truth of God to men, or man's worship back to God.

One basic reason why Reformed Christians want nothing in their worship that is not commanded by God is because they know themselves to be sinners by nature. When a man has little appreciation of this truth, he may feel that he can invent something that will add value to Christian worship. He may feel, for example, that he can write a hymn that will improve the worship service by expressing a thought that he feels has been neglected. But when a man understands his own unworthiness before God he will not imagine for one moment that he can improve on the inspired psalms of God. Nothing but the inspiration of the Holy Spirit, in other words, can qualify a man to contribute a hymn to the Church of God for use in divine worship. And we know (from the Bible itself) that no man today has this divine inspiration (Rev. 22:18-19).

Reformed Christians sometimes (and quite wrongly) have an inferior feeling. Because of the simplicity of their worship—or in other words, because they do not have some of the things that are common in other churches, things that are attractive to human nature—they almost apologize for not having those things that are not commanded. What Reformed Christians should realize is that adherence to this principle does not make them the poorer. To the contrary, it is their true riches. For what could be more wonderful than to receive from the Lord himself a sure knowledge of *the way that He would be worshiped*? And what could be a higher privilege than to observe—and to keep pure and entire—all such religious worship? It is quite possible, of course, to abuse even such a precious thing as this. This is what we would do if we were satisfied to simply have the form of godlines while denying the power thereof! It is for this reason that we must be on our guard. We must not assume that God is pleased with us just because we have a pure *form* of worship. Nor are we to assume that God cannot accept others merely because they do not have a pure form of worship. After all, no church is perfectly pure even in its form of worship. And whenever God accepts sinners it is in spite of their sin and imperfection. So God may well be more pleased with those who have sincere and repentant hearts, even though their form of worship is less pure, than with those who have a purer form of worship but are less zealous in heart. Nevertheless, we ought to strive for nothing less than a pure worship that is also zealous. And it would be a great mistake to say that this matter of pure worship is unimportant so long as man is sincere in heart. If such were the case then God would not have given us this second commandment.

What, then, are the great benefits of keeping a pure worship of God? In answer to this question we notice that it is in this commandment that God mentions children. When this commandment is violated, in other words, it is the children that suffer the most. This is not difficult to understand. When we bring in these things that God has not commanded, our children do not understand that they are learning to worship God in a wrong way. They do not realize, in other words, that they are being influenced by things that have a human origin rather than a divine origin. This becomes a barrier to the power of the gospel and the working of the Spirit. But when we "receive, observe, and keep pure and entire all such religious worship and ordinances as God has appointed in his word," then God shows mercy in a remarkable way. In this event, the children are influenced by the truth. They do not learn to think of God as men have imagined that He might be. They have rather learned to think of Him as He has shown himself actually to be. Thus it is that the children are blessed in a particular way in a church that strives to keep the worship of God pure and simple as commanded in His word.

Let us, then, grasp this simple principle once and for all—true worship consists of the things that God has commanded in His word. What God has not commanded is therefore forbidden.

24

Questions:

1. How do Roman Catholics and Lutherans treat this second commandment?
2. In order to do this what adjustment do they find it necessary to make?
3. If this view were correct, what important matter would be left unattended in the ten commandments?
4. What is the great principle contained in this commandment?
5. In your own words state how the Reformed and non-reformed views differ.
6. Why did God give us a *principle* to tell us what is forbidden, rather than a specific list?
7. Do Presbyterian and Reformed churches always remain true to the Reformed view? Prove.
8. Do great works of human art help or hinder true worship? Why?
9. What do Reformed Christians find in themselves that makes them want to add nothing to what God has commanded in worship?
10. Why are Reformed Christians sometimes apologetic?
11. What should be their attitude? Why?
12. Does a pure form of worship by itself guarantee that God will be pleased with our worship? Explain.
13. What is one of the great benefits of keeping this commandment? Can you explain why this is true?
14. For your own thought: what are some things God has commanded in His worship? What are some things God has not commanded?

Question 51. What is forbidden in the second commandment?

Answer: The second commandment forbiddeth the worshipping of God by images,[1] or any other way not appointed in his word.[2]

Question 52. What are the reasons annexed to the second commandment?

Answer: The reasons annexed to the second commandment are, God's sovereignty over us,[3] his propriety in us,[4] and the zeal he hath to his own worship.[5]

1. Take ye therefore good heed unto yourselves, (for ye saw no. manner of similitude on the day that the Lord spake unto you in Horeb out of the midst of the fire): lest ye corrupt yourselves, and make you a graven image, the similitude of any figure, the likeness of male or female (Deut. 4:15,16).
2. What thing soever I command you, observe to do it: thou shalt not add thereto, nor diminish from it (Deut. 12:32).
3. O come, let us worship and bow down; let us kneel before the Lord our maker (Ps. 95:6).
4. . . . he is thy Lord, and worship thou him (Ps. 45:11).
5. But ye shall destroy their altars, break their images, and cut down their groves . . . for the Lord, whose name is Jealous, is a jealous God (Ex. 34:13,14).

Since there is no commandment that is more commonly violated today, we now consider some of the ways in which this commandment is disregarded.

The second commandment is broken when men attempt to make a graven image or a picture of the Lord Jesus Christ. The Bible teaches us that there is one God. It teaches us to worship three persons, the Father, the Son, and the Holy Spirit, as one God, the same in substance, equal in power and glory. But Paul tells us that we "ought not to think that the Godhead is like unto gold, or silver, or stone graven by art and man's device" (Acts 17:29). And Isaiah the prophet asks, "to whom will ye liken God? or what likeness will ye compare unto him?" (Isa. 40:18). No wonder Jeremiah the prophet says, "every man is brutish in knowledge . . . confounded by the graven image, for his molten image is falsehood . . . vanity, and the work of errors" (Jer. 10:14).

Now there was a time when Protestants recognized this evil. They saw the images in the Roman Catholic Church and they understood that this was a violation of the second commandment. They realized that this was wrong—this making of images and likenesses of Christ—even though the Roman Catholic Church was careful to say that it did not want people to worship these images, but only to worship the Lord *through* these images. But now, it seems, many Protestants have accepted the Roman Catholic position. They may not realize this. And they may still think, in their minds, that there is an important difference between a statue (image) and a picture (likeness). But the commandment recognizes no such difference. It forbids us to make any likeness, just as it forbids us to make any image, of the Lord.

One great argument has always been used in defense of these images and pictures of Jesus. It is the argument that they are useful as a reminder of Him, or (in the case of children) as a means of instruction. Against this we believe the following facts to be conclusive. (1) We do not know what Jesus actually looked like. We do not, then, as a matter of fact, have any true likeness of His physical appearance. When an artist paints a picture, out of his own imagination entirely, and then says, "This is a picture of Jesus Christ," he lies. And the picture is "falsehood . . . and the work of errors" (Jer. 51:18). (2) When we make such a representation we imagine the human nature of Jesus Christ to be separated from His divine nature. It is quite true, of course, that Jesus Christ is man. But He is also God. And He is God and man in one person. We may not at any time separate the one nature from the other. "All men should honour the Son," therefore, "even as they honour the Father" (John 5:23). (3) When we make a representation of Jesus Christ we also dishonor the Holy Scriptures. For it is "the holy scriptures" that "are able to make" us "wise unto salvation" (II Tim. 3:15). By the Scriptures *alone* the man of God is thoroughly furnished. We do not need to supplement the Scriptures with pictures of Jesus. (4) And it is by the Holy Spirit that we are enabled to so understand the Scriptures that we behold "as in a glass the glory of the Lord" (II Cor. 3:18). As Jesus himself promised, "when the Comforter is come . . . he shall glorify me: for he shall receive of mine, and shall shew it unto you" (John 16:14). Thus, when we make a representation of Christ, we dishonor the Holy Spirit. For it is His glory to show us the Savior.

It was John Calvin who said, "daily experience teaches, that the flesh is never satisfied, till it has obtained some image, resembling itself, as an image of God." Perhaps it is because of this strong desire in us to have a visible representation that God has given us the sacraments. "It appears to me extremely unworthy," says Calvin, therefore, "to receive any other images than those natural and expressive ones, which the Lord has consecrated in His Word: I mean baptism, and the supper of the Lord."

One of the arguments for these pictures, as we stated above, is that they are needed in order to instruct our children. Yet it is to be noted that God mentions children as one of the important reasons for *not* using such pictures. The reason for this is evident: we all tend to accept as true and right whatever we learn from our parents and teachers. If *they* do not tell us that these pictures and images are evil, then we are going to have the feeling that they are good. This is what *has* happened in most Protestant churches in the last few generations. Pictures of Jesus first came in through the pages of the Sunday School materials. Little by little the children became accustomed to them. They grew up with the feeling that these pictures of Jesus were good. Now, these same people—in adult life—are bringing these pictures into the worship services. Stained glass windows are being brought in, so that people can see familiar pictures of Jesus (falsely so-called) while they worship. To illustrate this we print the following form used a few years ago in a United Presbyterian church, at the dedication of stained glass windows in the place of worship.

Minister: To the glory of God the Father; to the service of Jesus Christ and His Church; and to the quickening influence of the Holy Spirit.

People: We dedicate these windows.

Minister: To ever remind us of the spirit of friendliness and generosity that prompted the gift of these beautiful windows to this church and community; and with a prayer to God that we, the members of this church and congregation, may ever emulate the same spirit.

People: We dedicate these windows.

Minister: For the ministry of art to the soul; for the inspiration of the design of these windows to the intellect; and for the direction of the thoughts of the congregation in channels of Christian meditation.

People: We dedicate these windows.

Minister: For the beneficent influence of the figure of Christ in the presence of the congregation in the hours of worship; and for

28

the quiet, unobtrusive influence of windows during the week; and for the good of the whole community.

People: We dedicate these windows.

Minister: For the continual, winsome invitation suggested by these pictures to accept the wholesome and vital teachings of Jesus; and for the suggestion that we ever seek to know the truth; and practice the faith, hope, charity, prayer, joy, love, and peace in our daily lives.

People: We dedicate these windows.

It will be clear to any discerning person that pictures of Jesus are a far greater evil than is commonly realized. But we do well to remember that this is but one way in which this commandment can be broken. It is broken whenever we introduce into the sphere of religious instruction and worship that which has no basis in God's Word. And we only need to visit many Protestant churches today to see how much there is that is commonly accepted in worship today that has no biblical foundation.

Come, let us visit one of our large Presbyterian churches. Here, in the youth room we see what is called a "worship center." There in the center is—not a Bible—but an altar. There are candles burning. Above the altar is a picture of Christ. Before it we see the bowed heads of the children whose forefathers suffered much in order to be delivered from such things. But now we hear the great organ playing. The service is about to begin. So we hurry to the "sanctuary." Here we listen—as the poor people sit in rapture—to an organ concert. The processional begins. People slowly march in. They are dressed in special religious robes. They look very pious. They are carrying things, such as a gold cross, and lighted candles. When they are all in place, a spot light is turned on. And suddenly the minister enters. He is dressed in a black robe and wearing a red cape about the neck. But there is hardly time for the sermon. These other movements have taken too much time. The sermon is a short talk about daily life, with some good advice. Then, with much the same concert atmosphere, the recessional follows. People go out feeling light-hearted and uplifted—much as one feels when he has seen a good movie, or heard a concert. And no one realizes that there has been a violation of the second commandment in this service almost from beginning to end!

In contrast to this, the unadorned simplicity of worship as envisioned by the authors of the Catechism is striking. And it becomes more and more noticeable as the vast majority of Protestant churches have moved in a Rome-ward direction. But let us resolve that we will not be moved from this high standard. Let us vow to the Lord that we will strive to maintain a pure and simple worship. And let us do so secure in the knowledge that God has commanded us to do it. Let us remember that He is God, and that we are His subjects. But most of all let us rejoice in the assurance that if we will do this, God will not fail to confer rich spiritual benefits upon our children, and our children's children. For this is the promise attached to this second commandment.

Questions:

1. What is perhaps the most common violation of the second commandment today?
2. Why is it wrong to make a picture of Jesus?
3. What is the main argument for such? Answer this argument.
4. Did Calvin allow any visible representation of Jesus? Explain.
5. Why is it particularly dangerous to use pictures of Jesus to teach children?
6. How is this illustrated in the form of dedication? (Underline, and be ready to read phrases that bring this out clearly.)
7. "But I do not worship this image, or picture!" Show this argument wrong.
8. What are some of the violations of this commandment in the large Presbyterian church described above?
9. What are some arguments for maintaining simple (and pure) worship?
10. Can you explain why (or how) this will especially benefit the children?

LESSON SEVEN

Question 53. Which is the third commandment?

Answer: The third commandment is, Thou shalt not take the name of the Lord thy God in vain; for the Lord will not hold him guiltless that taketh his name in vain.

Question 54. What is required in the third commandment?

Answer: The third commandment requireth the holy and reverent use of God's names,[1] titles,[2] attributes,[3] ordinances,[4] and works.[5]

1. Give unto the Lord the glory due unto his name (Ps. 29:2).
2. Extol him that rideth upon the heavens by his name JAH (Ps. 68:4).
3. Who shall not fear thee, O Lord, and glorify thy name: for thou only art holy (Rev. 15:4).
4. Keep thy foot when thou goest to the house of God, and be more ready to hear than to give the sacrifice of fools" (Eccles. 5:1).
5. I will worship toward thy holy temple, and praise thy name for thy loving-kindness and for thy truth: for thou has magnified thy word above all thy name (Ps. 138:2).
6. Remember that thou magnify his work, which men behold (Job 36:24).

The third commandment teaches us the *attitude* required in true worship. Just as it is wrong to worship a false god (the first commandment), or to worship the true God in a wrong manner (the second commandment), so it is of no avail to worship the true God—in the right way—without a sincere heart (the third commandment). "Now therefore fear the Lord, and serve him in sincerity and in truth" (Josh. 24:14). It is in this way that we must understand the third commandment.

"O Lord, our Lord," says the Psalmist, "how excellent is thy name in all the earth" (Ps. 8:1). What the Psalmist means is that God's name is not a mere word—not an empty title. No, God's name means something. And it means something *because* God has revealed his name in all the earth. The whole world is a revelation of the meaning of God's name. Just as the name Rembrandt has meaning because of the great paintings that he has produced,

31

so God's name has meaning because of His works of creation and providence. We do not really know God's name, in other words, until we learn His fame! This is what Jesus meant when he said, "I have manifested thy name unto the men which thou gavest me out of the world" (John 17:6). Jesus revealed God the Father to the disciples. This He did by doing the great works of God before them. From this we see that God's name really includes everything that reveals God as He really is. The Bible reveals God as He really is. It does this because it records for us, without error, the revelation that God has made of himself. Names such as Lord, Father, Creator, etc., are a part of that revelation. So are titles, such as omnipotent, Counsellor, Comforter, etc. We learn that God is holy, merciful, just, etc. And we hear His word, and (through the record of Scripture) learn of His works. All of these help us to understand what it means to say God, or Lord. It is when we learn to know God as He really is, and *then* speak His name, that we begin to understand what this commandment is concerned to teach us.

The popular view is that a man takes God's name in vain only when he uses that name in a profane manner. We say that God's name is taken in vain when men swear or curse. And, of course, this *is* an example of taking God's name in vain. People will sometimes excuse themselves on the grounds that they do not really mean it when they use God's name this way. They will say that they do not even realize that they are using God's name—they do it without even thinking. But this is the very thing that the third commandment condemns. The word "vain" means exactly this: carelessly or without thought. It means to use a very important word as if it had no high and holy meaning.

But let us not imagine that this is all that the third commandment teaches us! No, in order to understand the meaning of this commandment more clearly we need to ask a question. What does it mean to *take* God's name? Literally it means to "lift up" that name. It means that we lift up the name of God and identify ourselves with Him. We can illustrate this by thinking of what a woman does when she marries. She *takes* her husband's name. If she really means it when she takes her marriage vows, she takes her husband's name permanently ("till death do us part," she will say). She does not take his name in vain! In a similar way, a Christian will confess his faith before men. He will vow—or swear—before men that he takes Jesus Christ as Lord and Savior. And it is this, above all, that the third commandment is concerned with. We must be certain—when we confess our faith—that we really mean it. We must be certain that we do not take His name in vain! "Be not

32

rash with thy mouth," says the Bible, "and let not thine heart be hasty to utter any thing before God: for God is in heaven, and thou upon earth; therefore let thy words be few. When thou vowest a vow unto God, defer not to pay it; for he hath no pleasure in fools: pay that which thou hast vowed. Better is it that thou shouldest not vow, than that thou shouldest vow and not pay" (Eccles. 5:2-5). It is so easy to go through the motions, and say the words, without deep sincerity of heart! It is easy to have the form of Godliness, while denying the power thereof!

We must realize, however, that no person is completely free of the sin of taking God's name in vain. For in order to keep this commandment perfectly as Christians, it would be required that we never hear—or say—the word God, or Jesus, without deep sincerity and reverence. This would mean that we would never let our minds wander as we pray—that we would always pay attention to the sermon in church—and so on. And the truth is that we are all —at times—very much like Shorty as we see him in the illustration here. We see Shorty seated in the family pew at church. The minister is preaching about the wonderful works of God. Shorty ought to be listening. He ought to be concentrating all his attention on the Word. But his mind is wandering to other things—the things that concern his own personal pleasure—rather than the things belonging to the worship of God. And so, because he is not concentrating his mind and heart on the worship of God (as he appears to be doing), he is really taking God's name in vain!

It will be clear by now that the third commandment—much more than the first or second—concerns the aspect of worship that *no one can discern except God*, and (with God's help) the individual believer. As we examine the doctrine taught in a particular church, for example, we can tell which God is being worshiped there (the first commandment). As we observe the practices of this church, we can determine the manner of worship (the second commandment). But only God can tell which person—or persons—in even the most faithful churches are really worshiping Him in heart! It is for this reason that the Catechism warns us that "however the breakers of this commandment may escape punishment from men, yet the Lord our God will not

33

suffer them to escape His righteous judgment." Think of Judas Iscariot. He professed to believe in the Lord Jesus Christ. He took part (outwardly) in worship that was rightly conducted. He seemed, in the eyes of men, a faithful disciple. No one could justly say that he worshiped a false god, or that he worshiped in a wrong manner. But since he did not have a sincere and believing heart, the Lord knew that his worship was in vain. Thus we see that this commandment has a special application to those who do attend faithful Christian churches. Such must be on guard lest they be satisfied with an outwardly correct religion, which does not live in the heart! The great lesson that we must learn is that there is no true religion, in God's sight, unless it is heart religion!

A final word needs to be said concerning the third commandment and the use of oaths. Some have imagined that a Christian may not swear at any time whatsoever. The words of Jesus are sometimes quoted in support of this view: "But I say unto you, swear not at all: neither by heaven, for it is God's throne; nor by the earth, for it is his footstool; neither by Jerusalem, for it is the city of the great King; neither shall thou swear by thy head . . . etc." (Matt. 5:34 f.). A careful reading of this entire passage will show that what our Lord was condemning was the common Jewish practice of swearing by all sorts of things (such as heaven, Jerusalem, etc.) other than the name of God. In this way, it was thought, one could swear as often as he wished and yet be guilty of no sin, because God's name was not being used. (This is much like those today who use words like "hell," or "damn," while avoiding the use of words like Jesus Christ, or God.) Jesus says that this *indirect* method of swearing is just as wrong, in principle, as direct swearing would be. No Christian should ever speak of hell, for example, without solemn thoughts of a just and holy God! But the point we wish to emphasize is this: it is proper to swear by God's own name when it is done for weighty reasons, and in a right manner. "Thou shalt fear the Lord thy God, and serve him," says the law, "and shalt swear by his name" (Deut. 6:13). It is for this reason that Christians should swear—take an oath—in a court of law, for example. It is for this reason that our covenanting Presbyterian ancestors solemnly swore adherence to the principles of Reformed Christianity. We ought to be very sure, when we swear, that we are doing so with God's approval—that what we affirm is true and right—and that we do so with a sincere heart. But when we do swear, we can know that God himself has promised His blessing (Ps. 15:4). This, after all, is what it means to witness a good profession before the world.

34

Questions:

1. With what is the third commandment concerned as respects true worship?
2. What does this commandment mean when it speaks of God's *name?*
3. Why does the word *Rembrandt* have meaning to most people?
4. Where do we learn to know God's name?
5. What does it mean, in the popular view, to take God's name in vain?
6. What does it mean to take God's name?
7. From the illustration of marriage how does a Christian take God's name in the highest sense?
8. Against what does Ecclesiastes 5:2-5 warn? Why?
9. Who is guilty of breaking this commandment? (How does Shorty illustrate this?)
10. Who can judge whether or not a person is breaking this commandment? Why?
11. Does this commandment forbid all swearing? Prove.
12. What does Jesus condemn in Matthew 5:34 f.?
13. Explain the significance of Psalm 15:4.

LESSON EIGHT

Question 55. Which is forbidden in the third commandment?

Answer: The third commandment forbiddeth all profaning or abusing of any thing whereby God maketh himself known.[1]

Question 56. What is the reason annexed to the third commandment?

Answer: The reason annexed to the third commandment is: that however the breakers of this commandment may escape punishment from men, yet the Lord our God will not suffer them to escape his righteous judgment.[2]

1. A son honoureth his father, and a servant his master: if then I be a father, where is mine honor . . . O priests, that despise my name? . . . and ye say wherein have we polluted thee? In that ye say, The table of the Lord is contemptible (Mal. 1:6,7). Ye have said, it is vain to serve God; and what profit is it that we have kept his ordinances (Mal. 3:14).

2. If thou wilt not observe to do all the words of this law that are written in this book, that thou mayest fear this glorious and fearful name, The Lord Thy God; then the Lord will make thy plagues wonderful . . . and of long continuance (Deut. 28:58,59).

In the previous lesson we learned that the third commandment requires the proper *inward attitude* in worship. It is for this reason that this commandment includes a special warning: "the *Lord* will not hold him guiltless that taketh his name in vain." It is not our place to judge the hearts of men. "For the righteous God trieth the hearts" (Ps. 7:9). So long as men profess the true religion, and outwardly conform to scriptural requirements, we are to regard them as true believers. Even though we may see faults and inconsistencies, we are to esteem others better than ourselves. Only when there is some outward evidence—such as embracing false doctrine, or openly disobeying the ordinances of God—are we to conclude that a person who has professed Christ's name has done so in vain! John says—concerning such persons in the Church in the time of the apostles—"they went out from us, but they were not of us; for if they had been of us, they would no doubt have continued with us: but they went out, that they might be made manifest that they were not all of us" (I John 2:19). Even an inspired apostle did not declare professing Christians guilty of taking God's name in vain, until they forsook the fellowship of the Church.

It will be evident, from this warning, that we need to be certain that we are sincere in our worship of the true God. It is for this reason that Scripture warns us against those types of religious life under which a basic insincerity may hide itself. (1) There is *formalism*, for example. This is what Isaiah condemned when he wrote: "The Lord said, forasmuch as this people draw near me with their mouth, and with their lips do honour me, but have removed their heart far from me, and their fear toward me is taught by the precept of men: therefore, behold, I will proceed to do a marvellous work among this people . . . for the wisdom of their wise men shall perish, and the understanding of their prudent men shall be hid" (Isa. 29:13,14). This is what the New Testament warns against when it speaks of "having a form of godliness, but denying the power thereof" (II Tim. 3:5). When people are born to all the privileges of a true visible church—knowing the doctrines of Scripture, and the scriptural manner of worship—they may imagine that they are worshiping God acceptably for this reason. But the Bible says that we must first know ourselves to be "wretched, and miserable, and poor, and blind, and naked" (Rev. 3:17). Only then—out of true repentance and faith—can we really worship God. (2) Somewhat similar to this is *traditionalism*. This was the sin of the scribes and Pharisees. They worshiped God "in vain," according to our Lord, because they taught "for doctrines the commandments of men . . . making the word of God of none effect" (Mark 7:7,13). The fifth commandment, for example, requires children to take care of their aged parents in their need. But what did these scribes and Pharisees do? They upheld a religious tradition which undermined the purpose of this commandment. They held that a man could devote his money to God. By saying "Corban" he would declare that everything belonged to God, as it were. Then, under cover of this seeming piety, he would no longer have any duty to take care of his parents! (It is interesting to note that the same wickedness has come into some branches of the Christian Church.) What we need to see is this: tradition often works against true heart religion. It tends to foster the idea that so long as we do something the way it has always been done that is the important thing. What we really need to ask ourselves, again and again, is this: is this really scriptural—am I doing this out of sincere devotion to God? (3) A somewhat different—but equally common—example, is *modernism*. Modernism is that name we give to a false version of the Christian faith. It

37

is that version which takes the *words* of the historic Christian faith and changes the *meaning* of these words entirely. In the historic Christian faith, for example, the word "resurrection" means the raising up again to life of a dead physical body. In the modernistic version this term is changed so that it means the continued influence of the teaching of Jesus Christ, or perhaps the on-going life of the soul when the body is dead. Even such important words as the names of the Savior are utterly denatured. To call Jesus *Lord*, in the biblical sense of that word, is to call Him Jehovah, or God. Thus when a modernist says "Lord, Lord," meaning only that Jesus was a great man, or teacher, this is precisely the taking of His name in vain.

It is little wonder, then, that Jesus said "not every one that saith unto me, Lord, Lord, shall enter into the kingdom of heaven." No, said Jesus, for "many will say to me in that day, Lord, Lord, have we not prophesied in thy name? and in thy name have cast out devils? and in thy name done many wonderful works? And then will I profess unto them, I never knew you: depart from me, ye that work iniquity" (Matt. 7:21-23). It is possible, in other words, that people will even deceive themselves. They will have the form—they will say the right words and do the right things—and therefore imagine that they also have the power of the true religion. This is because of two things. First, "the heart is deceitful above all things, and desperately wicked" (Jer. 17:9). This means we are prone to think better of ourselves than we ought. We do not like to think of ourselves as we really are. Secondly, there is the fact that Satan—the great deceiver—goes about seeking whom he may devour (I Pet. 5:8). His powers of deception are great (II Cor. 11:14,15). Thus it is that Scripture warns us again and again to take heed lest we be deceived (Matt. 24:4; I Cor. 6:9; Gal. 6:7; I John 3:7, etc.). And so we are commanded to examine ourselves to be sure that we do belong to Christ indeed (II Cor. 13:5).

How can we be sure, then, that we are not taking God's name (professing our faith in Jesus Christ) in vain? The answer is clearly stated by James: "be ye doers of the word, and not hearers only, deceiving your own selves. For if any be a hearer of the word, and not a doer, he is like unto a man beholding his natural face in a glass, for he beholdeth himself, and goeth his way, and straightway forgetteth what manner of man he was. But whoso looketh into the perfect law of liberty, and continueth therein, he being not a forgetful hearer, but a doer of the work, this man shall be blessed in his deed" (James 1:22-25). Here we see two important things. We see, on the one hand, the biblical description of a true Christian. That is what we might call a "word-picture" of what a professing Christian ought to be. Then, on the other hand, we have a professing Christian as he actually is. And the needful task is a careful—and constant—comparison of the two. Here we see why it is that

ARE THEY ALIKE?

Shorty's honest view of himself

The Bible portrait of a true believer

a true believer (but not a hypocrite) will constantly search the Scriptures. This does not mean that we are looking for a word picture of ourselves in the Bible. No, we are looking into Scripture in order to behold the glory of the Lord Jesus Christ into whose image we are to be conformed. "But we all, with open face beholding as in a glass the glory of the Lord, are changed into the same image from glory to glory, even as by the Spirit of the Lord" (II Cor. 3:18). As we behold this portrait in Scripture, we will come to see ourselves as we are. We will be humbled. We will be driven to earnest prayer to God for help. And we will be nurtured in our desire to be more like Him. The hypocrite, on the other hand, will be deficient precisely here: he will not live daily out of God's holy word!

It will be understood from the discussion above that a faithful Reformed church will take a solemn view of church membership vows. It is for this reason that such churches will insist upon careful instruction of those who desire to profess their faith. This is always true, but doubly imperative today, when it is common to have the form of the Christian faith, without the power. People must be taught to understand the things that differ, so that they can really understand what it means to take God's name. In the same way it is not the practice of faithful churches to allow people to come to the Lord's table upon the mere impulse of their own will. Faithful churches will admit none to the Lord's table until the rulers are satisfied that a proper profession of faith has been made. Churches that leave this responsibility entirely with the individual become guilty of encouraging people to take God's name in vain.

Taking God's name—or lifting it up in speech or profession—is an extremely important thing. We must never do it without realizing the solemn responsibility involved. Let it therefore be our constant aim to cultivate the utmost reverence for God—and His names—in the whole orbit of life.

Questions:

1. Why does this commandment include a special warning?
2. When should we esteem persons to be true believers?
3. When should we conclude that persons have been taking God's name in vain?
4. What is *formalism*?
5. How does formalism take God's name in vain?
6. What is *traditionalism*?
7. How does traditionalism work against heart religion?
8. What is *modernism*?
9. How does modernism take God's name in vain?
10. Why is it easy for us to be hypocrites?
11. How can we be sure that we are not hypocrites? How does the illustration show this?
12. What practices in faithful churches reflect a proper awareness of the meaning of this commandment?

LESSON NINE

Question 57. Which is the fourth commandment?

Answer: The fourth commandment is, Remember the sabbath-day to keep it holy. Six days shalt thou labour, and do all thy work: but the seventh day is the sabbath of the Lord thy God: in it thou shalt not do any work, thou, nor thy son, nor thy daughter, thy man-servant, nor thy maid-servant, nor thy cattle, nor thy stranger that is within thy gates: for in six days the Lord made heaven and earth, the sea, and all that in them is, and rested on the seventh day: wherefore the Lord blessed the sabbath, and hallowed it.

Question 58. What is required in the fourth commandment?

Answer: The fourth commandment requireth the keeping holy to God such set times as he hath appointed in his word; expressly one whole day in seven, to be a holy sabbath to himself.[1]

Question 59. Which day of the seven hath God appointed to be the weekly sabbath?

Answer: From the beginning of the world to the resurrection of Christ, God appointed the seventh day of the week to be the weekly sabbath;[2] and the first day of the week ever since, to continue to the end of the world, which is the Christian sabbath.[3]

1. Exodus 20:8-11 (quoted in Answer 57).
2. And on the seventh day God ended his work which he had made; and he rested on the seventh day from all his work which he hath made. And God blessed the seventh day, and sanctified it (Gen. 2:2,3).
3. Upon the first day of the week let every one of you lay by him in store . . . (I Cor. 16:2). And upon the first day of the week, when the disciples came together to break bread, Paul preached to them (Acts 20:7).

The Catechism teaches us that there are *ten moral* laws. Unlike *civil* and *ceremonial* laws given to the nation of Israel, these ten commandments are acknowledged to be God's will for all men in all ages. This truth is usually

41

admitted with respect to all the other commandments. But there are some who deny that this commandment (the 4th) is perpetually binding upon all men in all ages. Why, then, does the Catechism insist that this commandment too is moral? There are several reasons. (1) The first reason is that *the sabbath is a creation ordinance.* This means that this commandment did not come in at some later time in history, after many people had already lived and died. (We note that this *was* the case with the civil and ceremonial laws of Israel.) We know this because Genesis 2:2,3 clearly states the fact that God created the world in the space of six days, and then rested. Since man was made in God's image, it was for man's benefit that God "blessed the seventh day, and sanctified it" (Gen. 2:3). It is sometimes said that the sabbath commandment does not go back to the time of creation. Yet the commandment itself (Ex. 20:11) says that we are to remember the sabbath because "in six days the Lord made heaven and earth . . . and rested the seventh day: wherefore the Lord blessed the sabbath day, and hallowed it." The commandment itself claims a creation origin. Therefore we hold that it is binding for all men in all ages. (2) The second reason for saying that this commandment is moral is the fact that *God wrote all ten commandments on two tables of stone* (Ex. 31:18). God gave all the other laws and commandments to Israel through the hand of Moses. But these ten were given by His own hand. So God himself made a distinction between these ten commandments and all other laws. He showed us that these ten belong in a class by themselves. Since few will deny that most of these laws are moral (binding everyone everywhere), it would require very strong evidence to prove that this commandment is not moral. This we do not have. (3) The third reason for saying that this commandment is moral is the fact that *the New Testament nowhere teaches us that this commandment is abrogated.* Or, in other words, the New Testament does not say that we have no sabbath today. Jesus, speaking of the ten commandments, said, "think not that I am come to destroy [or abrogate] the law. . . . I am not" (Matt. 5:17). Paul says, "Do we then make void the law through faith? God forbid: yea, we establish the law" (Rom. 3:31). This is the constant teaching of the New Testament: the ten commandments of God do remain in effect. No doubt this is the reason why the early Christian Church kept a day holy to the Lord. It was the first day of the week (Matt. 28:1; Mark 16:2; Luke 24:1; John 20:1,19; Acts 20:7; I Cor. 16:2) which was observed as the sabbath.

But here we encounter what seems to be a difficulty: does not the fourth commandment speak of the *seventh* day? This is the argument used by such

42

sects as the Seventh-day Adventists. They say that the fourth commandment requires the observance of Saturday rather than Sunday as the sabbath of the Lord. They say this is necessary because Saturday is the seventh day, and not Sunday; and no one has the right to change this any more than they have the right to change any other commandment of God. In answer to this argument let us now look at our illustration.

Shorty says, "Six of these are for you, but the *seventh* is mine." But which

one is the seventh? The answer, of course, is that we will not know that until Shorty's friends take the first six apples. But *it could be any one of these* apples. When Shorty says that he will keep the seventh he simply means that one of the seven is his. So it is with God's command. The command itself does not tell us that we must keep the last day of the week as the sabbath. It only tells us that we must keep one day out of every week. The order of days is not fixed by the commandment itself. God fixed the order of days at the beginning when He created first (during six days), and then rested one day after the six had ended. God again fixed the order in a new way when He raised up Christ on the first day of the week, and began to call His Church together to worship on that day. But in either instance, it is equally true that six days are for work, and one day for worship. It is the *proportion* alone— and not the order—that is fixed by the commandment.

It is in the light of this distinction between proportion and order that we can also understand such texts as Colossians 2:16,17, Galatians 4:10,11, and Romans 14:5. Thus, for example, in Colossians 2:16,17 we read, "Let no man therefore judge you in meat, or in drink, or in respect of an holyday, or the new moon, or of the sabbath days: which are a shadow of things to come; but the body is of Christ." Now we know that there were men in the apostolic

43

period who wanted to perpetuate Jewish religious customs. Probably for this reason, the New Testament sabbath was, from a very early time, called "the Lord's day" (Rev. 1:10). And in common speech it was the Jewish observance which was called "the sabbath days." Since the Lord's Day—the first day of the week—was now the sabbath of the Christians, it was only natural that Paul should warn these Christians against being bound by any of these Jewish observances. For as soon as God himself changed the sabbath day from the last day to the first day of the week, the Jewish sabbath observance was no longer required. If we interpret these verses in this way, there is no conflict whatever between these verses and the known practice of the early Christian Church. The very reason Paul warned against observing the Jewish sabbaths, in other words, was because he himself gave commandment (I Cor. 16:2) concerning the first day of the week. There is nothing in the New Testament to show that sabbath observance is no longer required. Jewish sabbaths are no longer a part of God's ordinance. But this is only because we now have the Lord's Day. "There remaineth therefore a rest to the people of God" (Heb. 4:9).

Those who argue that there is no obligation to keep the Lord's Day as the sabbath of God usually argue that it still *is* a duty to attend the services of the Church. What they teach, in effect, is that the Church can require what God has not required. Thus observance of the Lord's Day becomes a duty in exactly the same way that it becomes a duty to observe "Good Friday" and "Christmas." Now this is the very thing that Paul so clearly condemned, when he said, "ye observe days, and months, and times, and years. I am afraid of you, lest I have bestowed upon you labour in vain" (Gal. 4:10,11). There is no power in the Church to require observance of days. God alone is the Lord of man's conscience. God alone can tell us that we must remember a certain day to keep it holy. And He has left our conscience free from the doctrines and commandments of men. It is for this reason that we must firmly believe that the fourth commandment too is a moral law of God.

Questions:

1. How many kinds of laws do we find in the Old Testament? Name them.
2. What are the three reasons for insisting that the 4th commandment is moral?
3. What do we mean by saying that this commandment is moral?
4. Which of these reasons seems most important to you? Why?
5. What is the argument of the Seventh-day Adventists?

6. What is the error in this argument?
7. How does the illustration bring out this point?
8. Can we rightly say that we keep the seventh day? Explain.
9. What is the true interpretation of such verses of Scripture as Col. 2:16?
10. What was the new sabbath day commonly called in the early Church?
11. What duty do those who oppose the teaching of our Catechism wish to retain? Upon what basis do they argue for this? Why is this wrong?
12. What was the wrong against which Paul protests in Gal. 4:10,11? Is it possible to conclude, from this, that we should not observe the popular "holy days"? Explain.

LESSON TEN

Question 60. How is the Sabbath to be sanctified?

Answer: The Sabbath is to be sanctified by a holy resting all that day, even from such worldly employments and recreations as are lawful on other days;[1] spending the whole time in public and private exercises of God's worship,[2] except so much as is to be taken up in the works of necessity and mercy.[3]

Question 61. What is forbidden by the fourth commandment?

Answer: The fourth commandment forbiddeth the omission or careless performance of the duties required,[4] and the profaning the day by idleness, or doing that which is in itself sinful,[5] or by unnecessary thoughts, words, or works, about our worldly employments or recreations.[6]

Question 62. What are the reasons annexed to the fourth commandment?

Answer: The reasons annexed to the fourth commandment are, God's allowing us six days of the week for our own employments,[7] his challenging a special propriety in the seventh,[8] his own example,[9] and his blessing the Sabbath-day.[10]

1. See Answer 57 (Lev. 23:3 also).
2. Exodus 16:25-28; Nehemiah 13:15-22.
3. Matthew 12:1-13.
4. Ye said also, Behold, what a weariness is it . . . and ye brought that which was torn, and the lame, and the sick . . . should I accept this of your hand? saith the Lord (Mal. 1:13).
5. They have defiled my sanctuary . . . and have profaned my sabbaths (Ezek. 23:38).
6. If thou turn away thy foot from the sabbath, from doing thy pleasure on my holy day: and call the sabbath a delight, the holy of the Lord, honourable: and shalt honour him, not doing thine own ways, nor finding thine own pleasure, nor speaking thine own words (Isa. 58:13).
7. See Answer 57 (and Ex. 31:15-16).

46

8. Ye shall do no work therein: it is the sabbath of the Lord in all your dwellings (Lev. 23:3).

9. It is a sign between me and the children of Israel for ever (Ex. 31:17).

10. And God blessed the seventh day, and sanctified it (Gen. 2:3).

The word *sabbath* means rest. It means a cessation of the activities proper to the other six days of the week, in order to sanctify—or set apart—one day to the Lord. It does not mean *rest* in the sense of inactivity (as in physical sleep). God rested after six days of creation, but He was still active in upholding the world by the word of his power. The contrast, then, is not between doing something and doing nothing. Neither is it a contrast between doing something sinful and something holy. This is not the meaning of "worldly employments and recreations." When the Catechism speaks of "worldly employments and recreations" it simply means those things that God calls us to do on the six days of the week appointed for this purpose. These are the things that we do to fulfill our task in the world—the task that we will one day lay down never to resume, because it is appointed to us to die and then be judged. Please observe that this does not mean that any part of life is non-religious. No, all of life is religious. But we are to worship God only, and we are to serve God too. This we are to do in the employments and recreations of this world. But then, once each week, we are to spend one day in a different kind of activity. And this, of course, is the worship of the Lord our God. We are to spend one whole day in this kind of activity, except for the works of piety, necessity, and mercy.

Now here we must pause to frankly admit that the Catechism sets forth a very lofty goal. For who can possibly reach such a high standard? Who can truthfully say that he has spent even one entire sabbath in the public and private worship of God? (And remember that this means avoiding even thoughts and words about our worldly employments or recreations.) No wonder the complaint is heard that this is much too difficult! No wonder it is said that this is an impossible goal! It *is*. For, as Catechism Q. 82 reminds us, "no mere man since the fall is able in this life perfectly to keep the commandments of God, but doth daily break them in thought, word, and deed." This is certainly true of the sabbath commandment. No man can say, "I have reached this goal." But this is no argument at all against the goal as such. And the Bible itself tells us that if we would know the "high places of the earth" and the "heritage" of the Lord, we must hold this high view of the keeping of the sabbath day. We should strive with all our might *towards* this high goal. Then, whenever we realize anew that we have come short of the

47

mark, we will thank God for the perfect work of Jesus Christ wherein alone we are saved.

But now let us consider the exceptions—the works of piety, necessity, and mercy—that ought to be done on the sabbath day. In the first picture we

see Shorty busy with a work of piety—a work that is done in order to facilitate the proper worship of God. He is helping to prepare the place of worship on a winter day in order that God's people might come together as He has commanded. If this work were not done, a spiritual duty would not be observed as it should. This is what Jesus meant when he said to the Jews, "have ye not read in the law, how that on the sabbath days the priests in the temple profane the sabbath, and are blameless?" (Matt. 12:5). The Levitical priests had to do certain work on the sabbath in order for worship to be observed. Thus we see that any work that may be required in order for divine worship to be observed on the Lord's Day is proper. We should realize, for example, that the Lord's Day is a day of hard work for the minister who preaches and teaches several times during that day. But it is not contrary to this commandment because it is a work of *piety*.

In this second picture we see Shorty performing a work of necessity. He is helping his mother by drying the dishes that must be done after dinner on the sabbath. In a similar way, Jesus and His disciples plucked the corn as they went through the fields (Matt. 12:1). When the Jews criticized this, Jesus said, "Have ye not read what David did, when he was an hungered and they that were with him; how he entered into the house of God, and did eat the shewbread . . ." (Matt. 12:3,4). The sabbath was not meant to stand in the way of man's nourishment. Thus when we do the things necessary for the proper preservation and sustenance of life, we do not violate this commandment. This is a work of *necessity*.

A work of *mercy* is clearly described by our Lord. "What man shall there be among you, that shall have one sheep, and it fall into a pit on the sabbath day, will he not lay hold on it, and lift it out?" (Matt. 12:11). And "how much . . . is a man better than a sheep?" (12:12). When a doctor has to operate to save a man's life, he is working; but he is not breaking the sabbath. When a fireman goes to put out a fire he too is working, but he is not breaking the sabbath. For a work of *mercy* is a part of keeping the sabbath day.

It is sometimes forgotten that the fourth commandment is *not* concerned with the sabbath only. It is concerned with all days. It not only tells us that we must keep one day holy to the Lord, but it also reminds us that we are to work six days as the servants of the Lord. This aspect of the commandment needs greater emphasis today, when so many people want "something for nothing," and when getting out of work seems to be the desireable goal. The Bible says "if any would not work, neither should he eat" (II Thess. 3:10). And we who are Christians ought, of all people, to be most diligent in work. For when we do our work faithfully, we also glorify God. But having said this, we yet need to keep the emphasis of the Catechism. God has allotted six days for our daily work. It is therefore the more evident that He has asked little enough when He designates one day for himself in a special way. How can we begrudge the Lord His sabbath, when He has given us six days for our daily employments and recreations? But the Lord knows our hearts. He knows that we are inclined by nature to forget—and to invent excuses to forget—the sabbath day. Thus He has given us His example (the Lord himself worked six days and rested one day) and His command, and has promised His blessing to those who will keep this commandment. So there is every reason to hold fast this day. Yet only the grace of God, by which the heart is changed, can make us turn from our own things on the sabbath day, in order to delight ourselves in God (Isa. 58:12,13). Herein is the essence of sabbath keeping, and hereby the sabbaths become a foretaste of the eternal sabbath above.

Questions:

1. What does the word *sabbath* mean?
2. Explain what is meant by rest on the sabbath.
3. What is meant by "*worldly* employments and recreations"?
4. Is life more religious on the sabbath than on other days? Explain.
5. Is worship the only proper activity for the sabbath? Explain.
6. Is it possible to keep the sabbath as the Catechism says it ought to be kept? Is this a valid argument against the Catechism teaching? Why?
7. Give an example of a work of piety (try to give your own original example).
8. Give an example of a work of necessity.
9. Give an example of a work of mercy.
10. Is the fourth commandment concerned with what we do on the sabbath only? Explain.
11. Why is the emphasis on the sabbath more than on the other six days in the Catechism?
12. What is the one source of inward agreement with the teaching of the Catechism (concerning the sabbath)?

Question 63. Which is the fifth commandment?

Answer: The fifth commandment is, Honor thy father and thy mother; that thy days may be long upon the land which the Lord thy God giveth thee.

Question 64. What is required in the fifth commandment?

Answer: The fifth commandment requireth the preserving the honour, and performing the duties, belonging to every one in their several places and relations, as superiors,[1] inferiors,[2] or equals.[3]

Question 65. What is forbidden in the fifth commandment?

Answer: The fifth commandment forbiddeth the neglecting of, or doing any thing against, the honour and duty which belongeth to every one in their several places and relations.[4]

Question 66. What is the reason annexed to the fifth commandment?

Answer: The reason annexed to the fifth commandment, is a promise of long life and prosperity (as far as it shall serve for God's glory and their own good) to all such as keep this commandment.[5]

1. Wives, submit yourselves to your own husbands, as unto the Lord (Eph. 5:22). Children, obey your parents in the Lord (Eph. 6:1). Let every soul be subject to the higher powers (Rom. 13:1).
2. And ye masters, do the same things unto them, knowing that your Master also is in heaven (Eph. 6:9).
3. Be kindly affectioned one to another with brotherly love: in honour preferring one another (Rom. 12:10).
4. Render therefore to all their dues (Rom. 13:7).
5. Honour thy father and mother: (which is the first commandment with promise) (Eph. 6:2).

All legitimate human authority is God-given. It is there because God has put it there. Thus the husband is given authority over the wife (Eph. 5:2). The parents are given authority over the children. And the duty to respect this authority is ultimately a duty unto the Lord!

51

When God created man the family was the only divine institution of communal life. After the fall of man, however, two other important institutions were given. These are the Church and the state. God gave the Church for the work of teaching the gospel and exercising a spiritual government over those who profess faith in Christ. The state was given in order to restrain lawlessness and evil in the world. We might diagram this as follows:

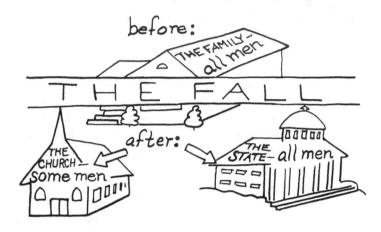

It will be evident, from the diagram, that the family is the archetype, and that the other institutions (Church and state) are based upon it. Had man never sinned the family would have been (to all intents and purposes) identical with both Church and state. That is, every member of the human family would—at the same time—have belonged to the same spiritual (Church) and political (state) body. It is sin which has disturbed this unity. Because of sin it has been necessary to introduce distinct areas of authority. Thus it is that we now have, in addition to the original God-given authority of parents, the *official* authority of rulers appointed in Church and state. We are commanded to obey our civil rulers (Rom. 13:1-7), and the elders and deacons in the Church (Phil. 1:1; Acts 20:28; Heb. 13:17). We might say that there is a divinely appointed extension of the original (parental) authority in both Church and state. Or we might say that God has instituted authority in Church and state after the pattern of parental authority. Perhaps this is why civil rulers are sometimes called fathers in the Bible (Isa. 49:23), and similarly the rulers of the Church (I Cor. 4:15). In any event, it is the obligation of Christians to honor and respect all God-given authority. It is this principle—

respect for, and obedience unto, duly constituted authority—that this commandment teaches.

It is important to realize, however, that *no one has absolute authority except God*. He alone is "Lord over all." (In our diagram, for example, God alone has complete authority over family, state, and Church.) All authority delegated to man by God is limited to that sphere ordained for it by Him. Thus there are family matters in which the state has no right whatever to meddle. There are Church affairs in which the state may not interfere. And, again, there are state affairs in which the Church is not competent to intrude. This limitation of authority is a most important principle, and it is one that is often violated today. It is violated when, for example, the state seeks to control the education of our children. The Bible clearly teaches us that this belongs within the sphere of parental authority (Deut. 6:6-15; Eph. 6:4). Parents are commanded to educate their children in the Lord (that is, with God's Word as the all-conditioning influence). But the Church today frequently invades the proper sphere of the state too. This is what happens when Church synods attempt to make all sorts of pronouncements on political matters. These are, of course, only examples. But they remind us of the fact that this great principle is often violated. Christians are therefore to be commended when they resist this evil by organizing communally. Family controled Christian schools are a worthy example.

We see, then, that there will be times when *Christians will have to resist the abuse of God-given authority*. When Jewish authorities commanded Peter and the other apostles to stop preaching, Peter said, "we ought to obey God rather than men" (Acts 5:29). When any person with authority (such as parent, minister, governor, etc.) transgresses the limits placed upon his authority—and intrudes upon the proper authority of another—then the Christian may resist, and ought to resist. This is what the Covenanters did in Scotland. They refused to submit to an unwarranted attempt (by the king) to impose religious compromise on the Church. When force was used against them in this illicit way they resisted with force. Luther followed the same principle when he resisted the tyranny of the pope of Rome. He saw that when the pope goes against the Scriptures, he no longer has any true authority and it is therefore right to resist him. All divinely conferred authority is limited, in other words, and it is our duty to respect and obey it only so long as it operates within the sphere appointed by God. From this it will be clear that much of our present-day "civil disobedience" is not Christian at all (even though it often claims to be). It is not Christian to insult civil rulers. It is

53

not Christian to break laws merely because we do not like them. The Bible clearly teaches that resistance is legitimate only at that point where the authority is transgressing the scriptural limits. A Christian must obey all laws, for example, except those that are directly contrary to the Bible. Even though there may be heavy burdens, and many things that we cannot approve in the affairs of our government, we still must give tribute and honor (as Christ did when He commanded that taxes be paid to Caesar). When we are compelled to disobey man in order to obey God, then this is what we must do. But even then, we must continue—in all other possible ways—to show due honor and respect.

In concluding our discussion of the fifth commandment, we note that it contains "a promise of long life and prosperity (as far as it shall serve for God's glory, and their own good,) to all such as keep this commandment." We have seen that this commandment is not primarily concerned with individuals. We are not to think, then, that every individual who strives to keep this commandment will enjoy a long life. We are rather to understand this commandment to mean that preservation of God's covenant people as a continuing community will depend upon their fidelity to this command. In other words, when we (as God's covenant people) live under a strong sense of God-given authority (in family, Church, and nation) we will be preserved by the Lord. But when we become careless and indifferent about this principle of God-given authority the result will be the loss of those blessings which can be ours only when these institutions are strong. When parents no longer teach their children to obey them, for example, it is no surprise that they grow up to have little or no respect for those who hold office in Church or state. When the family fails the Church is weakened, and the nation struggles to control the violence of its citizens. It is this, we believe, that helps to bring human totalitarian government upon men. It is truly a punishment from God. True totalitarianism is that which acknowledges God alone as supreme: His word alone is final in every sphere of life: and every human authority is subordinate to Him. When men no longer acknowledge God, they are punished by an enforced totalitarianism. In the Middle Ages it was the Church that became dictatorial and tyrannical. Today it is often the state. But the only real hope is a mighty revival of Reformed Christianity, with strong covenant family life. Only out of such God-dominated families will there be the spiritual strength to resist human totalitarianism. For only out of such families will there come people who are ready to exercise God-given authority in every sphere of life under the absolute sovereignty of God.

Questions:

1. Why do we have human persons with authority over other human persons?
2. What are the three most basic institutions regulative of human life?
3. Which was original? Why were the others given later?
4. Does the 5th commandment apply to all of these spheres? Why?
5. What important principle is violated by state control of education?
6. Give another example of the violation of this same principle.
7. May Christians ever resist persons having God-given authority? If so, when?
8. Is present-day civil disobedience biblical? Explain.
9. Is the promise attached to this commandment individual or communal? Explain.
10. What causes the rise of state-totalitarianism?
11. Why does stronge covenant-family life work against this?

LESSON TWELVE

Question 67. Which is the sixth commandment?

Answer: The sixth commandment is, Thou shalt not kill.[1]

Question 68. What is required in the sixth commandment?

Answer: The sixth commandment requireth all lawful endeavours to preserve our own life,[2] and the life of others.[3]

Question 69. What is forbidden in the sixth commandment?

Answer: The sixth commandment forbiddeth the taking away of our own life,[4] or the life of our neighbour unjustly,[5] or whatsoever tendeth thereunto.[6]

1. Exodus 20:13.
2. So ought men to love their wives as their own bodies, for no man ever yet hated his own flesh: but nourisheth and cherisheth it (Eph. 5:28,29).
3. Defend the poor and fatherless: deliver the poor and needy (Ps. 82:3,4).
4. Paul cried out with a loud voice, saying, Do thyself no harm (Acts 16:28).
5. Whoso sheddeth man's blood, by man shall his blood be shed (Gen. 9:6).
6. If thou forbear to deliver them that are drawn unto death, and those that are ready to be slain: if thou sayest, Behold, we know it not: doth not he that pondereth the heart consider it? (Prov. 24:11,12).

We can only understand the sixth commandment when we realize that man was made in God's image. It is because man is God's image that we may not murder any man. We say this for the following reasons: (1) The Bible does not say that it is murder when we kill animals. It is true, of course, that before the time of the flood of Noah, animals were not given to man for food. But after the flood they were (see Gen. 1:30; 9:3). So even though the killing of animals be a result of man's fall, the Bible makes a clear distinction between these two kinds of killing. (2) Again, we note that when Cain committed the first murder (Gen. 4:8), the blood of his brother Abel cried out from the ground for vengeance (Gen. 4:10). Yet, because Cain himself was made in God's image, no individual was to take it upon himself to punish Cain (Gen. 4:15). (3) When God did command that murderers be put to death (and

56

this was after the flood), the reason given was that man was made "in the image of God" (Gen. 9:6). So the great principle that we must grasp is that murder (the unjust killing of a human person) is wrong because man was made in the image of God.

Having said this, however, it is equally important to stress the fact that *it is not always an act of murder when a human life is taken by another person*. This can be clearly seen from the fact that when God gave Moses these ten commandments, He also gave him an inspired interpretation of these ten commandments in the books of the law (Exodus, Leviticus, Numbers, and Deuteronomy). In this divinely inspired interpretation we clearly see that there are times when it may be necessary to kill a human being in order to keep this commandment. "If a thief be found breaking up," says Exodus 22:2, "and be smitten that he die, there shall no blood be shed for him." This means that when a prowler tries to break into my house, I have the duty to try to protect my family from the harm that this person might do to them. And if, in this just defense of life, the life of the prowler be taken, it is not a case of murder. It is, in other words, the thief alone who is at fault and he alone who caused the violence resulting in his own death. We also see in the Bible that this same principle applies to nations. If a foreign nation tries to enter the territory of our nation to harm and destroy, it is the duty of the rulers of our nation to take military action against them (Rom. 13:1-7). For the civil ruler (whether king, or president, or prime minster) "beareth not the sword in vain: for he is the minister [servant] of God, a revenger to execute wrath upon him that doeth evil" (Rom. 13:4). Sometimes Christian people have thought it wrong to kill even in defense of their country. But when a Christian is called to serve his country in army or navy, and called to do so in a just cause, it is not at all against the sixth commandment to do so. For in this situation the Christian is acting, not as a private person who kills for no just reason, but as a proper agent of the government. And God himself has given power to the government for this very reason. Indeed, *if the government did not use this power then it would be guilty of breaking this commandment!* For instead of keeping the innocent from being killed, it would—in effect—be allowing (and therefore helping) the murder of these weak and innocent ones. Here too we can see the wickedness of those who argue against capital punishment. Capital punishment simply means the killing (or execution) of those who are guilty of murder. We believe that capital punishment is right simply because God commands it in the Bible (Gen. 9:6) Those who argue that capital punishment simply adds one murder (execution of the criminal) to another (the one already committed by the criminal) confuse two entirely different things. When a man takes the life of another unjustly, that is murder. But when the state takes the life of a murderer who is guilty, that is not murder. When the state does not take the murderer's life it becomes guilty of failing to protect the innocent. For it is often a fact that the murderer is free to kill again.

It must not be thought, however, that the sixth commandment has only to do with direct acts of violence. No, the commandment also "requires all lawful endeavors to preserve" life, and forbids "whatsoever tends" to the destruction of life. And here we can perhaps illustrate pictorially. In Figure A we see

FIG. A: ENDANGERING LIFE   FIG. B: PRESERVING LIFE

something that is all too common. People risk their lives needlessly just for a thrill. They engage in dangerous sports knowing that there is a serious risk of death. But whenever the Christian thinks of "flirting with death" or "daredevil" stunts, and the like, he ought to remember the sixth commandment. And he ought to say, "No, I must not do anything that even tends towards the destruction of life." For this reason Christians have refused to support such sports as bull fighting. There is just no need for such a risk of life. In Figure B we see the other side of the matter. Here we see Shorty removing a source of real danger to a little infant. This is an example of doing something that tends to preserve life. (Many other examples will immediately come to mind.)

58

But let us go on to notice that it is in this sixth commandment that we have God's rule for a temperate life. Many Christians maintain that, in addition to the ten commandments, we also need a rule forbidding the use of certain material things. (Some would even go so far as to forbid the drinking of coffee!) This is not the teaching of Scripture. "I know, and am persuaded by the Lord Jesus," says Paul, "that there is nothing unclean of itself" (Rom. 14:4). *No material thing is evil in itself.* It is only the abuse of material things that is wrong. (And any material thing can be abused.) This is the reason that Scripture constantly warns against intemperance in anything! Intemperance means excess, over-indulgence. And temperance means a moderate use, or a restricted use. So whenever a Christian uses anything, he must do it in such moderation that it does not tend to the destruction of life. He does not need an additional commandment, then, because this sixth commandment is the commandment of God having to do with temperance. It is the commandment of God which forbids *the abuse of anything.* Whenever the Church has made a list of forbidden things, it has only made it more difficult for its members to clearly understand this commandment. For true temperance has to do with all things, not just some things. And it is the individual himself who must exercise his conscience and judgment in the use of things. No church can really take that responsibility for him!

Finally, it must not be thought that the sixth commandment is complied with if we merely "live and let live." For the essence of all the law of God is to love the Lord with all that is in us, and our neighbor as ourself. It is not enough, then, that we seek to do our neighbor no ill. We must rather seek to do him good. And we must remember that life is more than meat and drink, and death is more than the mere dissolution of the body. The Christian, in other words, knows that Christ came in order that we might have life everlasting. The Christian therefore must exert himself in order to seek eternal life for those who are in the way of death. If our neighbor is on the way to destruction, and we do not make any attempt to warn him, are we not guilty then of the most heinous violation of this commandment? "Let him know that he which converteth the sinner from the error of his way *shall save a soul from death*, and shall hide a multitude of sins" (James 5:20). This is to keep the sixth commandment in the highest sense of the word!

Questions:

1. Why is it wrong to kill (or murder) a human being?
2. Is it wrong to kill animals? Why?

3. Is it wrong to kill a man in self-defense? Prove.
4. Is it wrong for a nation to engage in war? Explain.
5. Is it wrong for a Christian to kill on behalf of his government? Explain.
6. Why would a government be guilty of murder if it did not use military power for national self-defense?
7. Why is capital punishment right? Prove.
8. Does a government become guilty when it does not retain capital punishment? Why?
9. Give your own example of something that endangers life.
10. Give your own example of something that tends to preserve life.
11. Does the Bible contain a commandment that regulates temperance? If so, what commandment is it? Explain.
12. What does *temperance* mean?
13. In the use of what things must a Christian be temperate?
14. What is the highest duty involved in this sixth commandment?

Question 70. Which is the seventh commandment?

Answer: The seventh commandment is, Thou shalt not commit adultery.[1]

Question 71. What is required in the seventh commandment?

Answer: The seventh commandment requireth the preservation of our own,[2] and our neighbour's chastity,[3] in heart,[4] speech,[5] and behaviour.[6]

Question 72. What is forbidden in the seventh commandment?

Answer: The seventh commandment forbiddeth all unchaste thoughts,[7] words,[8] and actions.[9]

1. Exodus 20:14.
2. Flee also youthful lusts (II Tim. 2:22).
3. While they behold your chaste conversation coupled with fear (I Pet. 3:2).
4. Whosoever looketh on a woman to lust after her hath committed adultery with her already in his heart (Matt. 5:28).
5. Let your speech be always with grace, seasoned with salt (Col. 4:6).
6. I Peter 3:2 (as above).
7. Matthew 5:28 (as above).
8. Neither filthiness, nor foolish talking, nor jesting, which are not convenient (Eph. 5:4).
9. Fornication, and all uncleanness, let it not be once named among you (Eph. 5:3).

Someone has well said that the worst is the corruption of the best! So we begin our consideration of the seventh commandment—the law of sex—by emphasizing the fact that sex desire, and the proper satisfaction of it, is not wrong. This is evident from the account of creation. When Adam was first created "there was not found an help meet for him [that is, a mate fit for him]" (Gen. 2:20). And it was God who said, "it is not good that the man should be alone: I will make an help meet for him" (2:18). Then, when God had created Eve and brought her to Adam, he prophesied, saying, "therefore shall a man

61

leave his father and his mother, and shall cleave unto his wife: and they shall be one flesh" (2:24). Thus we see that even in a sinless state there was the sexual urge. It was divinely created. And there was nothing evil in it then, for we read that "they were both naked, the man and his wife, and were not ashamed" (2:25). From this we learn that sex desire is not wrong in itself. Neither is it wrong to satisfy or fulfill this sex desire if this is done in the way that God has ordained. The Bible frankly recognizes the fact that it is this need which draws people together in marriage.

What the Bible condemns is simply the unlawful satisfaction of the sex urge. This means any sex relations outside the God-ordained state of marriage. In other words sex relations, except with a person to whom one is lawfully married, is sin. And though it is unpleasant to discuss the way in which the sex desire has become perverted and corrupted by sinful men, this we must do because the Bible itself does so. We can also see, from biblical teaching, that the tendency of the sinful human heart is to ever more wicked things. (1) There is first of all, the sin of *fornication*. "If a man find a damsel that is a virgin, which is not betrothed, and lay hold on her, and lie with her, and they be found; then the man that lay with her shall give unto the damsel's father fifty shekels of silver . . ." (Deut. 22:28,29). The Bible goes on to say that the man, in such a case, has the responsibility to marry the young woman with whom he has committed fornication. "Because he hath humbled her, he may not put her away all his days" (v. 29). But even though this is not as heinous a sin as those next to be mentioned, it is sin because it is contrary to God's ordinance. God's ordinance is that marriage should first be contracted, and then the sexual relationship begun. (2) Much more serious, however, is the sin of *adultery*. Under the law of Moses fornication was not punished with death. Adultery *was*, as we see in the following text: "if a man be found lying with a woman married to an husband, then they shall both of them die, both the man that lay with the woman, and the woman" (Deut. 22:22). The only exception mentioned by Moses is the case of a woman who is forced against her will. (3) Much worse still is the wretched sin of *bestiality*. "Whosoever lieth with a beast shall surely be put to death" (Ex. 22:19). This sin is called bestiality because it literally brings man into the category of beasts. We may perhaps feel ill even to think of such a vile thing. If this is true we ought to be thankful to God, who has made us feel such revulsion. But we need to realize that there are men today—very educated too—who want to see this sort of wickedness made legal in our land. (4) Yet wretched as this sin of bestiality is, it does not exhaust man's capacity for vile iniquity. No, the depth of abomination is found in the sin of *homosexuality*. "Thou shalt not lie with mankind, as with womankind: it is an abomination" (Lev. 18:22). This was the sin that was so rampant in the ancient Greek and Roman world. It is, sad to say, becoming a prominent thing in our time. In our society today there are many who are outspoken in their defense of this crime against heaven.

We do well, then, to realize the depths of sinful corruption to which men go. God recognized this, and therefore spoke out plainly about these sins in His Old Testament law. What we need to realize is that we ourselves are—by nature—inclined to these same sins. We need to realize that it is only by the grace of God that we ourselves can escape the corruption that is in the world (II Pet. 1:4). Let us consider, then, the way in which the Lord enables men to rule the impulse of sex to His glory, and their own good. (1) The Bible says that God gives to some the gift of *continency*. By this we mean that God enables some to live without having sexual relations, by giving them the strength to resist temptations to adultery. Jesus said, "there are some eunuchs, which were so born from their mothers womb: and there are some eunuchs, which were made eunuchs of men: and there be eunuchs which have made themselves eunuchs for the kingdom of heaven's sake. He that is able to receive it, let him receive it" (Matt. 19:12). Some are born without normal bodies, or minds. Some are injured in war, or locked up in prison so that they cannot have sex relations. But some, like Paul the Apostle, voluntarily live without sex relations. This does not mean that they have no sex desire. It means that they are able to rule over this desire for the sake of serving Christ more effectively—and the Lord gives them the strength to do this. (2) For others, however—and this includes most people—this is not possible. "Every man hath his proper gift of God, one after this manner, and another after that. I says therefore to the unmarried and widows, it is good for them if they abide even as I. But if they cannot contain, let them marry: for it is better to marry than to burn" (I Cor. 7:7-9). Thus, for most, marriage is the God-given means of controlling sexual desire. Even then, however, marriage must be "only in the Lord" (I Cor. 7:39), that is, between two believers. If a person is already married before becoming a Christian, *then* it is the duty of that person to remain married to the unbelieving husband or wife. As long as the unbelieving partner is willing to remain in the bonds of marriage, the believer may not depart. Only when the unbeliever is guilty of (a) adultery, or (b) desertion which cannot be remedied, can the Christian go free and marry another in the Lord (see I Cor. 7:10-12; Matt. 19:8). In addition, of course,

63

there are certain close relatives with whom one may not be married. (See Lev. 18 and 20; Mark 6:18; Matt. 14:4; I Cor. 5:1.)

Jesus said that "whosoever looketh on a woman to lust after her hath committed adultery with her already in his heart" (Matt. 5:28). From this we see that it is not the outward act alone which constitutes sin against the seventh commandment. No, it is the thought and intent of the heart as well. And it is the thought and intent of the heart *in the first place.* It is for this reason that we must *resist the beginnings* of the various sins that we have been discussing. We must make a covenant with our eyes. And we must be on guard lest we put ourselves in the way of the temptation of Satan. Let us try to illustrate what we mean.

Here we see Shorty **standing** in front of the magazine rack at the corner drug store. Here, sad to say, he sees all sorts of magazines that present material (nude pictures) that stimulate sexual desire. This is, of course, only one common example of the way in which temptation presents itself today. We could also discuss motion pictures, books, magazine articles, and so on. But the point is that we must seek to avoid temptation by refusing to even look at things that we know to be fraught with temptation. And it should never be forgotten that the world does not view sex as the Christian does. The world (that is, the prevailing attitude of society) does not regard sexual relations outside of marriage as the sin that they really are. So we must be on our guard.

But even more important: we, as Christians must fight evil with truth—and sin with righteousness. Here we see Shorty selecting a book from the church library which deals with sex from a biblical point of view. He is thus doing justice to his natural curiosity. But he is building a true picture of sex *and* a growing desire for a Christian marriage. Today, more than ever before, this kind of counter-action is important. Our society is more and more saturated with an anti-Christian view of sex. More than ever, then, we must overcome evil with good! And this is not only God's way, it is also the promise of God that this way will be blessed! (I Pet. 1:5-11).

Questions:

1. Is sex desire wrong? Prove.
2. When is sex desire wrong?
3. What is fornication?
4. What is adultery?
5. What is bestiality?
6. What is homosexuality?
7. Are these equally wicked? Why?
8. Is the Bible right to speak of these things? Why?
9. In whose heart will the tendency toward these sins be found?
10. What is continency?
11. For what reasons may men be continent?
12. What is required (by God's law) for those who have not the gift of continency?
13. Whom may a Christian marry?
14. What are valid grounds for divorce?
15. What does Figure A teach us?
16. What does Figure B teach us?

LESSON FOURTEEN

Question 73. Which is the eighth commandment?

Answer: The eighth commandment is, Thou shalt not steal.[1]

Question 74. What is required in the eighth commandment?

Answer: The eighth commandment requireth the lawful procuring and furthering the wealth and outward estate of ourselves[2] and others.[3]

Question 75. What is forbidden in the eighth commandment?

Answer: The eighth commandment forbiddeth whatsoever doth or may unjustly hinder our own[4] or our neighbour's wealth or outward estate.[5]

1. Exodus 20:15.
2. Provide things honest in the sight of all men (Rom. 12:17). Be thou diligent to know the state of thy flocks, and look well to thy herds (Prov. 27:23).
3. If thy brother be waxen poor, and fallen in decay with thee, then thou shalt relieve him (Lev. 25:35). Look not every man on his own things, but every man also on the things of others (Phil. 2:4).
4. If any provide not for his own, and specially for those of his own house, he hath denied the faith, and is worse than an infidel (I Tim. 5:8).
5. "Let him that stole steal no more: but rather let him labour, working with his hands the thing which is good, that he may have to give to him that needeth (Eph. 4:28).

The Bible clearly teaches us that God is the ultimate owner of all that exists. "The heavens are thine, the earth also is thine: as for the world and the fulness thereof, thou hast founded them" (Ps. 89:11). It is by the sovereign will of God, therefore, that man is given the right to property in responsible service to Him. At the beginning God said, "Behold, I have given you every herb . . . and every tree . . ." (Gen. 1:29). After the fall this is equally true. It is God who allots to various nations their portion of the earth (Acts 17:26). It is God who gives to different persons different abilities whereby they are able to gain a measure of wealth (Matt. 25:19-46). Thus the Scripture clearly requires that men use abilities and opportunities given to them by the Lord (Prov. 6:6-8).

The right of private property, then, is an ordinance of God. If it were not so the law would not say, "Thou shalt not steal." For how could anyone steal if men did not have the right to private property? You cannot steal something from a person unless that thing rightfully belongs to that person. It is for this reason (among others) that the Christian must oppose communism and socialism. Basic to socialism or communism is the idea that private ownership should give way to collective ownership. (Socialists would achieve this by peaceful means. Communists would use violent means whenever necessary to achieve this end.) But when everything belongs to everyone, then *nothing really belongs to anyone.*

Christians have sometimes felt a sympathy toward socialism or communism. And there are two reasons for this. (1) For one thing there have been great abuses in what we call a capitalist society. Men have sought to advance their *own* wealth and outward estate without regard for the welfare of others, and indeed, often at the ruthless expense of others. The fact that socialism and communism claim to eliminate these tendencies has sometimes deceived Christians. (2) Then too, there is a superficial similarity between these systems and the "sharing of all things in common" of which we read in the book of Acts. "And all that believed were together, and had all things in common; and sold their possessions and goods, and parted them to all men, as every man had need" (Acts 2:44,45). A close reading of this message, and a study of Acts 5:1-11, will show that this was not really similar to socialism or communism. For while it is true that, for a time, the early Christians shared all things in common, it is also true that they did so only on a voluntary basis. It was never required that anyone give up private property. And the inspired apostles always recognized this *right* of private property (Acts 5:4).

The Bible says there are *two* legitimate ways in which we may obtain property. (1) One is by inheritance (see Num. 36:7-9; II Cor. 12:14; Eph. 4:28; Phil. 4:18). We all receive our first possessions in this way. Our parents or guardians give us whatever property we possess. (2) The other way is by our own labor. "Let him that stole steal no more," says Paul, "but rather let him labor, working with his hands the thing which is good, that he may have to give to him that needeth" (Eph. 4:28). Wealth obtained in either of these two ways is not evil. People often say that money is the root of all evil. But the Bible says that the *love* of money is the root of all evil. If we secure our money in either of these two ways (mentioned above), and if we value

67

our money only as a means to serve God, then wealth itself is a blessing. Thus the book of Proverbs says, "Be thou diligent to know the state of thy flocks, and look well to thy herds . . . and thou shalt have goats' milk enough for thy food, for the food of thy household, and for the maintenance for thy maidens" (Prov. 27:23,27). It is only when we work diligently in order to secure adequate wealth that we will be able to fulfill our obligations. For, as the apostle says, "if any provide not for his own, and specially for those of his own house, he hath denied the faith, and is worse than an infidel." (I Tim. 5:8).

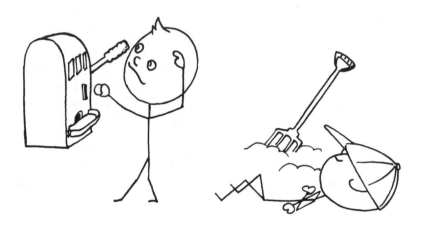

Stealing, then, may be defined as the unlawful obtaining of property. This means that (a) it is not given to us as a gift, and (b) we did not do anything to earn it by our labor. And it is not difficult to see how common this evil is. In Figure A we see Shorty considering a slot machine. This is a form of gambling. But it always involves the element of stealing because the motive is to get money without labor, and without it being given as a gift. When gambling involves a number of persons—and they all agree to "take a chance"—this essential element is not removed. It is still true that each is seeking to take what the others have without either of the above two conditions being met. We therefore hold that gambling is a form of stealing.

Another form of stealing is sloth. Here (in Figure B) we see Shorty taking a nap on the job. He has been hired to spade up this garden, and is being paid by the hour. But here he is taking time out when he is supposed to be working. This means that he is stealing. For it is stealing when we take money that is not given to us as a gift, without working for it in an honest and diligent way. This is becoming a great problem in our country today. There are even some people who will not work (though they could). They simply demand money from the government. Yet the Bible says, "If any would not work, neither should he eat" (II Thess. 3:10).

Another form of stealing is *waste*. The Bible says that a person who wastes is like a slothful person (Prov. 18:9). And this too is a very common thing today. Some workers treat the property of their employers with utmost carelessness. They do not treat *his* things the way they would treat their *own* things. And the result is that this costs the employer a great sum of money. This, according to the Bible, is a form of stealing.

Finally, let us mention fraud as a form of stealing. When we take advantage of the needs of men, or even their lack of understanding as to a fair price, so as to charge them more for a certain thing than it is worth, we are guilty of stealing. Thus, today, it is a common thing to use deceptive or misleading advertising and packaging. Various ways are used to make people think that they are getting more than they really are getting. Exorbitant claims are made for various products.

We cannot enumerate the many ways in which it is possible to break this eighth commandment. But we can say, with this commandment as well as the others, that we can best eliminate the negative by accenting the positive. "Servants," says Paul—and today we would say: employees—"be obedient to them that are your masters [we would say: employers] according to the flesh, with fear and trembling, in singleness of your heart, *as unto Christ*; not with eyeservice, as menpleasers; but as the servants of Christ, doing the will of God from the heart; with good will doing service, as to the Lord, and not to men: knowing that whatsoever good thing any man doeth, the same shall he receive of the Lord" (Eph. 6:5-8). It is only when we realize, in other words, that our work too is really service to God—done primarily to please Him—that we will have the antidote to stealing, as employees. And the same is true of those who are employers. "And, ye masters, do the same things unto them . . . knowing that your Master also is in heaven; neither is there respect of persons with him" (Eph. 6:9). The time is overdue in our nation when Christian people should stand up and be counted. The need is urgent for Christians to apply biblical principles to labor-management problems. An example that is worthy of imitation is the *Christian Labor Association of Canada* (it is often called CLAC). Here we see workers considering not only their own things—or rights—but also the things of their employers. They are saying that it is just as important to work faithfully, to the glory of God, as it is to obtain a fair wage, etc. This is not only right, but we are convinced that it will be blessed of the Lord. There will be far greater wealth, in the end, as a result of keeping the eighth commandment (and this means for both employer and employee) than ever there could be through self-centered efforts to steal in various ways.

Questions:

1. What is the ultimate source of the right of private property?
2. Can it be proved that one man has a right to more than another? Explain.
3. What is the basic tenent of socialism and communism as respects property?
4. Why have Christians sometimes felt a sympathy toward such systems?
5. Have men violated the eighth commandment in the name of capitalism? How?
6. Explain the difference between socialism-communism and Acts 2:44,45.
7. What are the two legitimate ways in which we may secure property?
8. Give an example of each.
9. Is it wrong to be rich? Prove. Is it wrong to seek to be rich? Explain.
10. What is stealing?
11. Why is gambling a form of stealing?
12. Why is sloth a form of stealing?
13. Why is waste a form of stealing?
14. Why is fraud a form of stealing?
15. Can you think of other forms?
16. What is the best antidote to the sin of stealing?
17. Do we need such organizations as the CLAC? Why?

LESSON FIFTEEN

Question 76. Which is the ninth commandment?

Answer: The ninth commandment is, Thou shalt not bear false witness against thy neighbour.[1]

Question 77. What is required in the ninth commandment?

Answer: The ninth commandment requireth the maintaining and promoting of truth between man and man,[2] and of our own[3] and our neigbour's good name,[4] especially in witness-bearing.[5]

Question 78. What is forbidden in the ninth commandment?

Answer: The ninth commandment forbiddeth whatsoever is prejudicial to truth,[6] or injurious to our own[7] or our neighbour's good name.[8]

1. Exodus 20:16.
2. Speak ye every man the truth to his neighbour (Zech. 8:16).
3. Having a good conscience: that, whereas they speak evil of you, as of evil-doers, they may be ashamed that falsely accuse your good conversation in Christ (I Pet. 3:16).
4. Demetrius hath good report of all men, and of the truth itself . . . (III John 12).
5. A faithful witness will not lie (Prov. 14:5).
6. With their tongues they have used deceit (Rom. 3:13).
7. God forbid that I should justify you: till I die I will not remove mine integrity from me (Job 27:5).
8. He that backbiteth not with his tongue, nor doeth evil to his neighbour, nor taketh up a reproach against his neighbour (Ps. 15:3).

The God of the Bible is a God of truth. He is called "Lord God of truth" (Ps. 31:5). God cannot lie (Titus 1:2). And because it is our duty to be perfect even as our Father in heaven is perfect (Matt. 5:48) so are we to tell the truth at all times. As the Apostle John has said, "No lie is of the truth" (I John 2:21). No lie is really in accord with God who is truth! For it is not God, but only Satan, who is the father of lies (John 8:44).

71

But what is truth? This is the question Pontius Pilate asked, and it has been asked again and again since man fell in Adam's transgression. God created man to think his true thoughts after Him. So long as man accepted God's Word and obeyed His command, he knew and spoke only the truth. But when the Devil deceived man he began to try to find the standard of judgment, or truth, in his own reason. He was thus the victim of the lie of Satan, and could not speak the truth. As Jesus once said to the unbelieving Jews: "Ye are of your father the devil, and the lusts of your father ye will do. He was a murderer from the beginning and abode not in the truth, because there is no truth in him. When he speaketh a lie, he speaketh of his own: for he is a liar, and the father of it" (John 8:44). Truth, then, is that which is in accord with the mind of God. And it is only the regenerated person—the person who repents and believes—who can again learn to speak the truth. Jesus is the way, the truth, and the life. It is only when we are in union with him that we can really know the truth. This does not mean that the converted person will, as soon as he is converted, arrive at perfection in his knowledge of, and obedience to, the truth. No believer, in this life, perfectly attains unto truth. But he does come to know truth, and he does attain to a more and more perfect conformity to the truth.

In order to speak the truth, then, two things are essential. (1) First, it is necessary that we speak *what we sincerely believe* to be the truth. We cannot say that a person is truthful if he himself does not believe what he is saying. (2) But it is also necessary that we speak *what actually is*. We cannot say that a person is telling the truth unless he speaks what is in accord with existing reality. It is not enough, in other words, that we simply repeat something *as true*, which we have heard from others. For this reason the Bible condemns gossip. "Thou shalt not go up and down as a talebearer among thy people" (Lev. 19:16). The godly man does not take up "a reproach against his neighbour" (Ps. 15:3). He doesn't believe everything he hears, especially when it is an evil report. Before he tells anyone else he wants to know whether or not it really *is* true.

But is it necessary to tell the truth at all times and in every situation? Or are there certain circumstances that justify deception? There are some who say that lying can be right in some instances. (1) Thus people speak of *little white lies*. This is what we have in a false politeness and flattery. People say what other people want to hear, rather than what is true. They say, "my but you are handsome," or, "what a beautiful singing voice you have," when it is not so. The basic thought is that since these "lies" do not

72

do any harm but rather make people feel good, they are therefore harmless and innocent. But the Bible says "no lie is of the truth" (I John 2:21). And "the Lord shall cut off flattering lips" (Ps. 12:3). (2) Other people say that there is no harm in what we may call *lies of convenience*. Thus someone may call one the telephone. It may be a person that we do not want to talk with. So in order to avoid something very unpleasant, we may say: "Tell them that I am not at home." We feel that we are justified because it would do more harm to talk with this person, and get into an argument, and so on. But again, we note, the Bible says that we may not do evil that good may come. We are not allowed to commit an act that is against the law of God in order to avoid a possible future evil (Rom. 3:8). (3) But the most commonly defended "lie" is the so-called *lie of necessity*. There are times, it is argued, when we simply *must* lie! And for this, it is said, even Scripture support can be found. Did not Abraham lie to save his own life? (Gen. 12:13, 19; 20:2, 5, 12). Did not the midwives lie to Pharaoh? (Ex. 1:19, 20). Therefore—it is argued—we too

73

may lie in time of war, or danger. But this is not a sound argument. Abraham also committed adultery. But this does not justify adultery. In order to prove that lying can be right, we would have to prove that Abraham not only lied, but lied with God's approval. And this we cannot prove. We can prove that God permits us, in dire circumstances, to conceal (or withhold) part of the truth from those who are our enemies. We see this from God's command to Samuel (I Sam. 16:1-5). God commanded Samuel to do *two* things. But when the king demanded to know what he had done, God instructed Samuel to tell about one of the things that he had been doing, but not the other. So he was to tell that part of the truth that would do no harm, and to conceal that part of the truth that would result in harm if it were told. *But observe*: he was not permitted to lie. In other words, while God does say in effect, that evil men may not have a right to know all truth that we could tell, He does not say that we have the right to tell them any lies.

The Catechism mentions "witness-bearing" as a special concern of the ninth commandment. This means there are certain times and circumstances when the sin of lying (which is evil at all times) is even more heinous than at other times. If we are called as witnesses in a court of law, for example, we are charged by duly appointed authority to tell the truth, the whole truth, and nothing but the truth. The very fact that the oath is necessary in such instances is a reminder of the fact that we are too careless, ordinarily, as respects the truth. Yet, as Jesus taught us, we ought to learn to speak, in our daily conversation, in such a way that truth has the same priority with us at all times, as it would for unbelievers in a solemn trial in a court-room (Matt. 5:33-37). Let us conclude our study of the ninth commandment, then, with a brief consideration of some ways in which we can study greater obedience. (1) One of the things that we can do is to *think before we speak*. "In the multitude of words there wanteth not sin: but he that refraineth his lips is wise" (Prov. 10:19). We need to learn what an unruly member the tongue is, and we need to know what a great fire it can ignite (James 3:5). At the same time we need to remember that (2) *silence can be* as *wrong* as any evil speaking. If we know that a wrong has been done and do not speak up, we are guilty when our very silence will seem to express our consent (Lev. 5:1). (3) Perhaps the chief need is to consider *God*, rather than man, as *the one that we must please*. So much of what we say is really calculated to please people. We want to win their approval, or gain some advantage from them. But when a man realizes that nothing really matters except to please God, then his speech will change radically. This reminds us that there is only one way that

74

we can ever learn to speak the truth. It is by a saving relationship to the Lord Jesus Christ. He is the way, the truth, and the life. And no man can obtain the truth except in Him.

Questions:

1. What is truth? Can God lie? Can Satan tell the truth? Why?
2. Are we, by nature, able to tell the truth? Why?
3. What two elements are necessary if we are to tell the truth?
4. Can you give an example in which the first of these elements is missing?
5. Can you give an example in which the second of these elements is missing?
6. What kind of untruths are often accepted as right by men?
7. Which of these may be made to seem to have scriptural support?
8. How can it be shown that this is not genuine scriptural support?
9. Is it always necessary to tell the whole truth? Prove.
10. Is it more necessary (so far as God is concerned) to tell the truth in a court of law, than in ordinary conversation in daily life? Explain.
11. What are some of the ways in which we can strive to overcome the sin of lying?
12. Where must we get the desire and strength to tell the truth?
13. In your own way try to explain why it is wrong to gossip.
14. Is it wrong to flatter people? Why?
15. Can silence be a form of lying? Explain.

LESSON SIXTEEN

Question 79. Which is the tenth commandment?

Answer: The tenth commandment is, Thou shalt not covet thy neighbour's house, thou shalt not covet thy neighbour's wife, nor his manservant, nor his maidservant, nor his ox, nor his ass, nor anything that is thy neighbour's.[1]

Question 80. What is required in the tenth commandment?

Answer: The tenth commandment requireth full contentment with our own condition,[2] with a right and charitable frame of spirit toward our neighbour, and all that is his.[3]

Question 81. What is forbidden in the tenth commandment?

Answer: The tenth commandment forbiddeth all discontentment with our own estate,[4] envying or grieving at the good of our neighbour,[5] and all inordinate motions and affections to any thing that is his.[6]

1. Exodus 20:17.
2. Let your conversation be without covetousness: and be content with such things as ye have (Heb. 13:5).
3. Rejoice with them that do rejoice, and weep with them that weep (Rom. 12:15). Let no man seek his own, but every man another's wealth (I Cor. 10:24).
4. Neither murmur ye, as some of them also murmured . . . (I Cor. 10:10).
5. For where envying and strife is, there is confusion, and every evil work (James 3:16).
6. Wherefore, laying aside all malice, and all guile. and hypocrisies, and envies, and all evil speakings (I Pet. 2:1).

The law of God requires more than mere outward conformity in visible actions. It also requires inward holiness or rectitude of heart. The tenth commandment reveals this in a special way. Whereas all the other nine commandments are concerned with both outward actions and inward desires, the tenth commandment speaks only of an inward state of the heart. No doubt this is the reason why Paul the apostle said: "I had not known sin, but by the law: for I had not known lust, except the law had said, Thou shalt not covet"

76

(Rom. 7:7). As a Pharisee, Paul kept the commandments outwardly to such an extent that he was, "touching the righteousness which is in the law, blameless" (Phil. 2:6). That is, in the eyes and estimation of men, he was not guilty of adultery, murder, stealing, etc. But here was the one commandment that spoke of *inward desire only*. And this led the apostle to see his own sinfulness within. For, as someone has said, this commandment "takes us down to the fountains of desire, and touches the most secret sources of unholy actions, words, and thoughts."

It would not be inaccurate to say that coveting is the root of all other sin. James says "every man is tempted when he is drawn away of his own lust [or covetous desire] and enticed. Then when lust hath conceived, it bringeth forth sin, and sin, when it is finished, bringeth forth death" (James 1:14,15). So, as Paul says, a "covetous man . . . is an idolater" (Eph. 5:5). Or in other words, if the sinful desire is there, then there is already a violation of all the other commandments at least in principle. Thus some have held that the first beginning of sin in Adam and Eve was covetousness (the sinful desire to eat the forbidden fruit). Then, when this desire was expressed outwardly, there was a simultaneous violation of all the other nine commandments.

But why does this commandment speak of such common possessions (house, wife, manservant, maidservant, ox, or ass) if it has such far-reaching implications? The answer is this: covetousness begins with a dissatisfied heart. It begins when we compare our own situation with that of another who has (or appears to have) more than we do! "Take heed," said Jesus, "for a man's life consisteth not in the abundance of the things which he possesseth" (Luke 12:15). Let a man once become dissatisfied with the portion God has given him, and he will then be tempted with a thousand other sins. And it can hardly be denied that this is a besetting sin today. We are constantly stimulated, by television, by advertisements, by easy credit plans, and so forth, to feel that we *must* have something newer, and bigger, and better! The "good life" is pictured as belonging to those who *have* everything. How different the thought expressed by the Apostle Paul. "I have learned in whatsoever state I am, therewith to be content. I know how to be abased, and I know how to abound: everywhere and in all things I am instructed both to be full and to be hungry, both to abound and to suffer need" (Phil. 4:11,12). This, then, is the biblical requirement: full *contentment* with what God has given us.

This does not mean that we should make no effort to improve our wealth and outward estate. The Bible says, "He becometh poor that dealeth with a slack hand, but the hand of the diligent maketh rich" (Prov. 10:4). Scripture

teaches us that God has given us abilities that we ought to use diligently. God also gives us the opportunities that come to us to use our abilities. It is therefore our duty to use both our abilities and opportunities fruitfully. But we must at the same time be content with the *limits* of both our ability and opportunity. And we are not to grieve when someone else is enabled to advance beyond what we are able (Gal. 5:26; James 3:14,16). There is a sense, in other words, in which men are *not* created equal. God himself gives more to one than to another. And it is our duty to accept our place as God ordains with humble and thankful hearts.

But how, it may asked, can we find true contentment. The answer is that we can never learn to be content until God himself becomes our reward. To Abraham God said, "*I am* thy shield, and *thy exceeding great reward*" (Gen. 15:1). This is the great truth that we need to discover (or re-discover). When God created man, he coveted nothing. He had no need to covet anything, because he had the infinite riches of God as his delight. When he was deceived by Satan, he began to seek his "chief end" in the creature (that is, in things, and in self). But *things* can never satisfy the heart of man. God himself has set "eternity in their heart" (Eccles. 3:11), so the temporal things cannot fill the emptiness that is in man. Thus the only *cure* for covetousness is to find eternal life through Jesus Christ. When a man does this, he no longer sees the treasures of this world as genuine treasures. Now the words of Jesus have profound meaning. "Lay not up for yourselves treasures upon earth, where moth and rust doth corrupt, and where thieves break through and steal: but lay up for yourselves treasures in heaven, where neither moth nor rust doth corrupt, and where thieves do not break through nor steal: for where your treasure is, there will your heart be also" (Matt. 6:19-21). The true believer, in other words, has a treasure that far exceeds the sum total of all the treasures of this world. He knows that this present world—and all that is in it—will be destroyed (II Pet. 3:12) before God makes new heavens and a new earth (3:13). But the true treasure will never be taken away. "If ye then be risen with Christ," says the apostle, "seek those things which are above, where Christ sitteth at the right hand of God. Set your affection on things above, not on things on the earth, for ye are dead, and your life is hid with Christ in God" (Col. 3:1-3). This is the cure for covetousness: it is to "covet earnestly the best gifts" (I Cor. 12:31) so that we more and more forget these "things."

We conclude this discussion of coveting with an important reminder. There is a spiritual law operative in God's kingdom whereby many of the first shall be last and the last first. If a person has but few abilities and opportunities in this life, in other words, there is still no reason why he may not have as great a reward in heaven as any person having many abilities and opportunities. On the other hand, if a person has many abilities and opportunities this in itself does not guarantee that the reward in heaven will be greater. In Christ's parable of the talents (Matt. 25:14-30) the man who received five talents— and used them well—received no greater commendation than the man who received two talents and used them well. To both of them he said, "Well done, good and faithful servant, thou hast been faithful over a few things, I will make thee ruler over many things: enter thou into the joy of thy lord." And what could be greater than this? Someone has said that we will receive—out of the infinite glory and wonder of God and Christ—all that we can possibly receive! We will receive as much of the infinite as we finite creatures can hold—just as a million people today can enjoy as much of the ocean as they want, and there is still so much more that they cannot possibly contain it! So it is this great vision of God as our chief end and delight—God as our exceeding great reward—and a genuine and ruling concern to enjoy Him forever, that is really the only basis for keeping this tenth commandment.

Questions:

1. What great difference exists between the tenth and other commandments?
2. Why was this the commandment that made Paul realize he was a guilty sinner?
3. Why is it possible for Paul to say that covetousness is idolatry?
4. How is the "good life" pictured in modern culture?
5. What is wrong with this picture according to the Bible?
6. Is it wrong to work hard to get ahead? Explain.
7. What are the limits that we must accept, and be content with, if we are to avoid coveting?
8. What is the basis of true contentment?
9. Why can wealth never satisfy the deepest need of man and bring true joy?
10. Is there a kind of coveting that is good? Explain.
11. What is the spiritual law that enables "the last to be first"?
12. Why will it be impossible for us to covet in the world to come?
13. Try to state, in your own words, why it is only the Christian who can even begin to keep this commandment!

LESSON SEVENTEEN

Question 82. Is any man able perfectly to keep the commandments of God?

Answer: No mere man since the fall is able in this life perfectly to keep the commandments of God[1] but doth daily break them in thought,[2] word,[3] and deed.[4]

Question 83. Are all transgressions of the law equally heinous?

Answer: Some sins in themselves, and by reason of several aggravations, are more heinous in the sight of God than others.[5]

Question 84. What doth every sin deserve?

Answer: Every sin deserveth God's wrath and curse, both in this life, and that which is to come.[6]

1. For there is not a just man upon the earth, that doeth good and sinneth not (Eccles. 7:20).
2. The imagination of man's heart is evil from his youth (Gen. 3:21).
3. The tongue can no man tame: it is an unruly evil . . . (James 3:8).
4. In many things we offend all (James 3:2).
5. He that delivered me unto thee hath the greater sin (John 19:11).
6. Cursed is every one that continueth not in all things which are written in the book of the law to do them (Gal. 3:10). Then shall he say unto them on his left hand, depart from me, ye cursed, into everlasting fire . . . (Matt. 25:41).

What is the main difference between true Christian teaching, and all false religious teaching (and corrupted Christian teaching)? It is this: *God alone* saves his people, and to him alone belongs the praise and glory. In every false or corrupt system of teaching, man (the sinner) is given at least some credit for attaining unto salvation. Furthermore, this difference is seen at every step. Thus true religion holds, not only that man is entirely dependent upon God's grace at the beginning of the Christian life, but that it is God's grace that is decisive throughout the Christian life. "For without me," said Jesus, "you can do nothing" (John 15:5). This important truth is clearly brought out in this section of the Catechism. Here we see that a person continues to sin even after he becomes a believer. Yes, he sins daily in thought,

81

word, and deed. He does not want to sin. He tries hard not to sin. But he always has to confess, as Paul the Apostle did: "the good that I would I do not: but the evil which I would not, that I do" (Rom. 7:19). This is true of even the strongest Christians. That is why we cannot find even one person mentioned in the Bible (except Jesus Christ) who reached entire perfection *in this life*. Every right thinking Christian must therefore have a constant sense of his own unworthiness, *and* of his entire dependence upon the Lord.

In the light of this truth—that no mere man is able to live a sinless life—we can understand the two great errors against which we need to be on guard. (1) The first is called *perfectionism*. It is the type of teaching which says a Christian believer can reach the place, in this life, where he no longer sins. We find this, for example, in the Roman Catholic idea of "the saints." It is said that some Christians have reached the place that they were holy. They not only reached perfection, but even went beyond. They did more than God required. The "extra" is called a work of supererogation, and results in "merits" deposited in the treasury of the Church. Ordinary Christians, then, can draw from these merits of the saints to make up what they lack. We find another example among some Protestant denominations, and in certain non-denominational and inter-denominational movements. Here the teaching is to this effect: if we completely surrender to God He will give us victory. Thus we often find such slogans as: "let go, and let God," or "the secret of the higher life," and so on. The basic idea is that some Christians, who "learn the secret" as it were, can attain to a kind of sinless perfection. Yet the Scripture clearly states that there is no man on earth who does not sin (Eccles. 7: 20). "If we say that we have not sinned," says John, "we make him [God] a liar, and his word is not in us" (I John 1:10). So we must beware of this error. (2) An equally deadly error is *antinomianism*. (It means to be against the law. Anti = against, nomian = law.) Since no one can keep God's law perfectly, it is said, and since Christ satisfied the law for us, we are therefore free from all obligation to obey God's commandments. Some antinomians hold a "two-man" theory of Christian personality. The Christian, they say, is really two persons. He is partly "the old man in Adam," and partly "the new man in Christ." Whenever the Christian sins, then, it is the old man who is to blame. The "new man in Christ" will say, "I can't help it that my old nature acts that way!" But the Bible says that a Christian is a "new creature" in Christ, and that he has put off the old man with his deeds (Col. 3:9). We do still have the motions of sin in our members (Rom. 7:5). And the effects of the old nature are indeed with us as Christians. But the two-personality view is wrong. A Christian will not be ruled by sin. Neither will he excuse himself when he does sin by blaming it on the old nature.

The true believer (against these two errors) will (1) continually strive to be obedient to God, and (2) constantly confess his remaining imperfection and sin. Because he desires to be holy he will say that he loves God's law. He will not find anything in the commandments of God to grieve him (Rom. 7:22; I John 5:3). He will even know that he has passed from death unto life because he seeks after entire perfection. But he will also be conscious at all times that he has not yet attained to the goal. He will therefore look to Jesus alone as his only righteousness before God (Rom. 7:24,25). Or, in other words, the true Christian makes progress in two respects—he actually becomes more and more holy in practice, and at the same time repents more and more and believes more and more in Jesus Christ alone as his only hope. Let us try to understand why this is so.

The more light and understanding a believer has (of the law as it has been fulfilled in Jesus Christ), the more he will realize how great, or how high, the perfection required by God really is. He will say, with the Psalmist, "I have seen an end of all perfection: thy commandment is exceeding broad" (Ps. 119:96). Just as we will see more clearly the spots on a garment when we bring it to greater light, so the Christian becomes more aware of his sin. Even though he may be living more and more in obedience, then, he can also see the sin that remains more and more clearly too. This is why some of the greatest Christians in the history of the Church have also been the humblest. They were not pretending to think lowly of themselves: they really did consider themselves to be unworthy. The reason is simply this: the true believer learns to measure himself by the true standard of God's absolute holiness. No wonder he can make progress in obedience, and at the same time become more repentant and more dependent upon Jesus Christ!

It would be hard to think of a statement less accepted today than this: "every sin deserves God's wrath and curse, both in this life, and that which is to come." Now, even the most terrible crimes are explained (and excused) in terms of mental illness, bad environment, etc. The death penalty has been abolished in many states. The criminal is now said to need treatment, not punishment. So the whole concept of absolute law (and consequently of guilt and punishment) is more and more lacking today. Indeed, we often see the law changed in order to accommodate those who have broken it. How important it is, then, to grasp the teaching of this part of the Catechism. It is truly a life and death matter. It is an absolute law that brings us to see our urgent need of Christ. It says: be ye perfect, even as the Father in heaven is perfect. But who is perfect? There is only one. So, while the law is a rule of obedience for the Christian (the rule which shows him how to show gratitude to Christ for salvation) it remains after, as before conversion, the means of fostering faith in Jesus Christ alone as the believer's righteousness and salvation.

Questions:

1. What is the central difference between true Christian teaching and all false (or corrupt) forms of religious doctrine?
2. At what step in the system of truth is this seen?
3. What is taught by the perfectionist error? Who teaches this?
4. What is taught by the antinomian error?
5. What error, regarding Christian personality, do some antinomians teach?
6. Cite a scripture text proving perfectionism to be wrong.
7. Cite a text showing antinomian teaching to be wrong.
8. What will a sound Christian hold in distinction from these two errors?
9. Is it possible to become more and more holy and yet (at the same time) more repentant? Explain.

10. Is it our duty to be perfect?
11. Why does a Christian trust more and more in Christ, if (at the same time) he is actually becoming more obedient to God in his daily life?
12. Why is it especially important to grasp the principle taught in this part of the Catechism in our day?
13. What do you think the result will be if we cease to believe in an absolute law (or, in other words, an absolute standard of holiness)?

LESSON EIGHTEEN

Question 85. What doth God require of us, that we may escape his wrath and curse due to us for sin?

Answer: To escape the wrath and curse of God due to us for sin, God requireth of us faith in Jesus Christ, repentance unto life,[1] with the diligent use of all the outward means whereby Christ communicateth to us the benefits of redemption.[2]

Questions 86 and 87 (see Vol. I).

Question 88. What are the outward means whereby Christ communicateth to us the benefits of redemption?

Answer: The outward and ordinary means whereby Christ communicateth to us the benefits of redemption, are his ordinances,[3] especially the word, sacraments, and prayer;[4] all which are to be made effectual to the elect for salvation.[5]

1. Testifying both to the Jews, and also to the Greeks, repentance toward God, and faith toward our Lord Jesus Christ (Acts 20:21).
2. Wherefore the rather, brethren, give diligence to make your calling and election sure: for if ye do these things, ye shall never fail (II Pet. 1:10).
3. Teaching them to observe all things whatsoever I have commanded you: and lo, I am with you alway, even unto the end of the world. Amen (Matt. 28:20).
4. And they continued stedfastly in the apostles' doctrine and fellowship, and in breaking of bread and in prayers (Acts 2:42).
5. I have planted, Apollos watered; but God gave the increase (I Cor. 3:6).

We have seen that all men deserve God's wrath and curse, and that there is salvation in Jesus Christ alone. "There is none other name under heaven given among men, whereby we must be saved" (Acts 4:12). No more urgent question can ever be asked by sinful men, therefore, than that which is asked in Question 85 of the Catechism. In answer to this question we find a twofold answer. First, there is what we may call the *inward* graces of repentance and faith. These we have already considered in our study of the *ordo salutis* (the order of the application of redemption). Except for infants dying in

86

infancy, and mentally defective persons, all of the elect repent and believe. The Holy Spirit so works in them that they are enabled to respond to the call of the gospel. But there are also *outward* means through which the benefits of redemption are ordinarily communicated to the elect. By this we mean the instruments (or channels) appointed by the Lord himself, through which the Holy Spirit usually works. In making this distinction between the *inward* and the *outward* (grace and means), the Catechism teaches us never to confuse the instrument used by God, and God who uses the instrument. At the same time, however, it reminds us that there is a divinely established relationship between the two. Let us Illustrate:

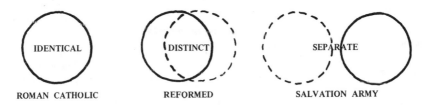

| IDENTICAL | DISTINCT | SEPARATE |
| ROMAN CATHOLIC | REFORMED | SALVATION ARMY |

The heavy circle represents the outward means. The broken circle represents the inward grace. In the illustration we see the three typical views. (1) In the Roman Catholic type the outward and inward are identical. The Church is seen as a storehouse of grace. The sacraments are outlets of grace much as electrical connections are outlets of electricity. Unless there is something faulty in the way in which the outward ordinance is administered and received, it is assumed that the inward grace is invariably present. Thus the Roman Church teaches baptismal regeneration, for example: *all* infants properly baptized (the outward) are therefore born again (the inward). This view is false and dangerous. It is essentially the view held by the Jews in biblical times who assumed that they were true sons of Abraham (inward) simply because they were circumcised (outward). But Paul said, "he is not a Jew, which is one outwardly; neither is that circumcision, which is outward in the flesh: but he is a Jew, which is one inwardly; and circumcision is that of the heart, in the spirit, and not in the letter; whose praise is not of men, but of God" (Rom. 2:18,19). (2) A very different view is held by such groups as the Salvation Army. They do not administer the sacraments at all. They hold regular worship services, but do not observe baptism or the Lord's Supper. From this it would seem evident that the outward means are deemed unimportant, and that the inward grace is not seen as having a divinely ordained connection with the outward means. It is not suggested that Salvation Army people cannot be true believers. This movement does emphasize the preaching of the word of God, and this is one of the appointed means of grace. But we do suggest that this is an unscriptural tendency: separating the outward and inward. The Lord himself commanded outward ordinances. He said to go into all the world to preach and administer the sacraments (Matt. 28:18,20). When the Church did this (Acts 2:42), "the Lord added to the church daily such as should be saved" (Acts 2:47). (3) The Reformed view says this: what God has joined together, let not man separate. There is a close, and divinely established, relationship between the inward and outward. God is not *tied* to His ordinances. He can work without them. The ordinances do not rule God; God rules the ordinances. But He uses them because He pleases. This enables us to understand two truths clearly taught in Scripture. a) On the one hand we see why the inward grace of God is *usually* seen in those who receive the God-given ordinances. Those who are blessed with faithful preaching, right administration of the sacraments, and faithful church discipline are usually people who have grace in their hearts. b) At the same time, on the other hand, it is not invariably so. Scripture mentions Simon (Acts 8:13) who heard the word and was baptized, but remained "in the gall of bitterness, and in the bond of iniquity" (Acts 8:23). We may not, therefore, take the inward grace for granted merely because we have the outward means. (Here we note, too, that since the Lord is not tied to the outward means, He can save infants dying in infancy, and others incapable of understanding the means.)

It will be clear, by now, that we must not undervalue the outward means. We must not suppose, for example, that we can neglect them without fear of harming ouselves. It is this insight which enables us to see the true importance of the visible Church. The true visible Church does three very important things: it preaches the word, administers the sacraments, and exercises discipline. Now there are no doubt some true believers in churches that lack these three distinguishing marks. We know that there will also be some hypocrites in even the most faithful visible churches. But let us not be so foolish as to minimize the tremendous difference between the faithful and unfaithful churches. Let us not imagine, in other words, that we can get along without a true visible Church. No, "for *there* the Lord commanded the blessing, even life for evermore" (Ps. 133:3). It is God himself who has ordained a blessing (inward) where His appointed means (outward) are maintained.

The Catechism speaks of *the diligent use* of the means of grace. **This** means that we may not expect the blessing of God when we neglect the ordinances of God. It is for this reason that we are warned, in Scripture, not to forsake the assembling of ourselves together (Heb. 10:25). And this is a lesson much needed today. Many people seem to imagine that the power of God is to be found in something rare or unusual. They therefore look for something special to give them a spiritual life. They hope for some famous evangelist to come to town—or they travel here and there looking for something new. But all the while they neglect the regular hearing of God's word preached, which is God's ordinary way of giving faith (Rom. 10:17). They neglect the sacraments, and even personal Bible reading and prayer. But here in the Catechism we learn that God's blessing is not found in the strange or unusual, but in the ordinary means of grace. That is why those who confess their faith and become communicant members of a sound Reformed Church are asked whether they will be faithful in attendance at the services of the Lord's Day. Jesus asid, "ask, and it shall be given you; seek, and ye shall find" (Matt. 7:7). But James adds the fact that we sometimes ask and receive not, because we ask amiss (James 4:3). What we need, then, is not only to seek eternal life, but to seek it in the right way. This we do when we seek inward grace in connection with (or by the diligent use of) the outward ordinances that the Lord himself has appointed. "Wherefore, the rather, brethren, give diligence to make your calling and election sure: for if ye do these things, ye shall never fall: for so an entrance shall be ministered unto you abundantly into the everlasting kingdom of our Lord and Saviour Jesus Christ" (II Pet. 1:10,11).

Questions:

1. Why is Q. 85 of the Catechism such an urgent question?
2. What are the two aspects of grace mentioned in the Catechism?
3. What is meant by each?
4. What is the Roman Catholic conception of the relationship between these two?
5. What is the Salvation Army conception?
6. What is the Reformed conception?
7. What scripture can you give to disprove these two false views?
8. What scripture would you use to prove the Reformed view?
9. What are the three marks of a true visible church?
10. Why is it important to belong to a true visible church?

11. Why does God's inward grace usually accompany His outward ordinances?
12. How do many today seek the inward saving grace of God? Why is this wrong?
13. Why does a sound Reformed church stress faithful church attendance?
14. Could a person dilligently use the outward means and not be saved?

LESSON NINETEEN

Question 89. How is the word made effectual to salvation?

Answer: The Spirit of God maketh the reading, but especially the preaching of the word, an effectual means of convincing and converting sinners,[1] and of building them up in holiness and comfort,[2] through faith, unto salvation.[3]

Question 90. How is the word to be read and heard, that it may become effectual to salvation?

Answer: That the word may become effectual to salvation, we must attend thereunto with diligence,[4] preparation,[5] and prayer,[6] receive it with faith[7] and love,[8] lay it up in our hearts,[9] and practice it in our lives.[10]

1. The law of the Lord is perfect, converting the soul (Ps. 19:7).
2. I commend you to God, and to the word of his grace, which is able to build you up, and to give you an inheritance among all them which are sanctified (Acts 20:32).
3. . . . the gospel . . . is the power of God unto salvation to every one that believeth (Rom. 1:16).
4. Blessed is the man that heareth us, watching daily at my gates (Prov. 8:34).
5. As newborn babes, desire the sincere milk of the word (I Pet. 2:2).
6. Open thou mine eyes, that I may behold wondrous things out of thy law (Ps. 119:18).
7. The word preached did not profit them, not being mixed with faith . . . (Heb. 4:2).
8. They received not the love of the truth, that they might be saved (II Thess. 2:10).
9. Thy word have I hid in my heart, that I might not sin against thee (Ps. 119:11).
10. . . . being not a forgetful hearer, but a doer of the work . . . (James 1:25).

Paul the Apostle once said: "Christ sent me not to baptize, but to preach the gospel" (I Cor. 1:17). The preaching of the word of God, then, has a cer-

91

tain priority. It is more important than the sacraments. Thus the Bible constantly reminds us that God uses "the foolishness of preaching to save them that believe" (I Cor. 1:21), and that "the gospel . . . is the power of God unto salvation" (Rom. 1:16) since "faith cometh by hearing, and hearing by the word of God" (Rom. 10:17). The reason is obvious: the sacraments *by themselves* do not convey a clear mesage to the ignorant and uninstructed man. A man who had never known about Christ could witness the sacrament of baptism and still know nothing about Christ, if he did not also hear the word with the sacrament. The sacraments depend upon the word. But the word is intelligible in itself. When the word is faithfully preached the explanation or meaning is self-evident! So God uses the word as the ordinary means of convincing and converting sinners. And let it be noted that it is *especially the preaching* of the word that God uses in this work. We can understand this if we remember that man, by nature, is dead in trespasses and sins. Among other things, this means that we cannot expect sinful men to take the initiative in discovering the truth. Scripture (Ps. 14; 53, etc.) shows us that men do not seek God, and do not discover the way of salvation for themselves. It is rather God who seeks men. It is God who comes to convince and convert them. That is why our Lord commanded His disciples to go into all the world to preach the gospel (Matt. 28:19,20). Faith usually comes by hearing, rather than by reading, for in this way God makes clear the fact that He alone is the author of our salvation. This does not mean that reading is unimportant, or that it is never used of God in convincing and converting sinners. In Acts 8:27-39 we read of the Ethiopian who rode along in his chariot reading the book of Isaiah. God then sent Philip to explain the written word to the Ethiopian. So both reading and hearing were used in this instance. Again, in Acts 17:11,12 we read of the Jews in Berea, who searched the Scriptures daily, as they listened to—and tested—the teaching of Paul. Reading of the Bible is thus seen to be very important too. But even in such cases, we notice that preaching is essential. It is the primary means.

But why is it that when the gospel is preached only some believe? The answer is that the gospel *itself* has no power to quicken the dead. Just as light has no power to give sight to the blind, so the gospel has no power to restore understanding to spiritually blind people. "It is the spirit that quickeneth," said Jesus (John 6:63). Without a direct work of the Holy Spirit in the heart, men may hear what the preacher says, and may even enjoy it; but they will never be convinced and converted. It was so with some who heard Ezekiel preach! "Lo, thou art unto them as a very lovely song of one that hath a pleasant voice," said the Lord, "and can play well on an instrument: for they hear thy words, but they do not do them" (Ezek. 33:32). This is what the Bible means when it speaks of having ears and not being able to hear. It means that people can hear the words (sounds) without appropriating them (the meaning). But when the Holy Spirit regenerates the heart the word has its effect. The Apostle Paul says (of the Thessalonian believers) "when ye received the word of God which ye heard of us, ye received it not as the word of men, but as it is in truth, the word of God, which effectually worketh also in you that believe" (I Thess. 2:13). Let us illustrate:

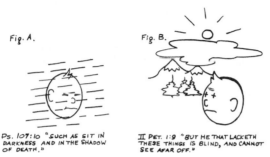

Fig. A.

Ps. 107:10 "SUCH AS SIT IN DARKNESS AND IN THE SHADOW OF DEATH."

Fig. B.

II PET. 1:9 "BUT HE THAT LACKETH THESE THINGS IS BLIND, AND CANNOT SEE AFAR OFF."

Both pictures represent men who have no saving faith. Both are in a condition of spiritual darkness or unbelief. But there is a great difference. For in the one case (Figure A) no light has arisen. No gospel has been preached to him. But to the other (Figure B) the true light now shines. The gospel has been preached to him. Observe too that the light has the power to drive the darkness away—the darkness that surrounds the sinner. But still, it does not have (of itself) the power to open his (spiritual, or inward) eyes that he might see. *This* is something that God alone can do. Thus we see that two things are necessary: the restoration of the light (through the gospel) and the restoration of the power to receive it (by a direct act of God within the heart).

It might seem, at first thought, that this would take away our responsibility. People might well say that it is not their fault if God does not regenerate their hearts. "If God will do this, then we will also believe," they might say, "but if He doesn't do this, then it isn't our fault if we cannot believe!" Our answer to this is simple: it is contrary to Scripture. Man's responsibility is not destroyed by reason of man's inability, nor by reason of God's regenerating grace. Thus it is that Jesus said to His disciples, "take heed therefore how ye hear: for whosoever hath, to him shall be given; and whosoever hath not, from him shall be taken even that which he seemeth to have" (Luke 8:18).

93

The disciples knew that the power to hear and understand the gospel was given by God. But Christ also taught them that they should exert themselves to be sure that they had this understanding! So the Catechism is right when it stresses our responsibility when we hear, and read, the word of God. One of the dangers that covenant children face is this: they are born into Christian families—instructed in the word—having a knowledge of the truth. It is therefore possible to mistake a mere passive conditioning for a saving faith. The gospel does not come to anyone with saving power unless there is a hungering and thirsting after Christ and His word. This is the reason why people who have received faithful gospel preaching for many years (in a passive way) will suddenly discover the power and wonder of that gospel in an entirely new way (when the Spirit quickens them).

The mind and heart are—sad to say—very forgetful. We can learn the doctrines of Scripture step by step, and then (in an amazingly short time) forget most of what we have learned. We are like the man who looks in the mirror and then immediately forgets what he looked like (James 1:23,24). We must therefore exert ourselves continually to lay the word of God up in our hearts and practice it in our lives. As newborn babes we must desire the milk of God's word (I Pet. 2:2). As mature Christians we must learn to digest the meat (Heb. 5:14). We must saturate ourselves with God's truth until we are "no more children, tossed to and from, and carried about with every wind of doctrine" (Eph. 4:14). Only in this way can we know that we ourselves have possession of God's truth in saving power.

Unless in Thy most perfect law
  My soul delight had found,
I should have perished at the time
  My troubles did abound.

Thy precepts I will ne'er forget;
  They quick'ning to me brought.
For I am Thine; O save Thou me;
  Thy precepts I have sought.

(Psalm 119, Part 12—Metrical Version)

Questions:

1. What is the most important means of grace? Why is this so?
2. Why does God use preaching more than reading as a means of grace?
3. What do such texts as Acts 8:27-39 show us?
4. Does the gospel have saving power unto all who hear it? Why?
5. What are the two essentials brought out in the illustration?
6. What does the teaching of the Catechism sometimes lead people to say?
7. Prove from Scripture that we are responsible.

8. Why is it important to stress this with regard to covenant children?
9. How can we know that we have experienced the power of the gospel?
10. Underline the words in the Psalm quotation which show that the Psalmist would have been lost without the word of God.
11. Circle the words in this quotation which show that regeneration was also essential.
12. Double-underline the words which prove that the Psalmist was indeed convinced and converted.

LESSON TWENTY

Question 91. How do the sacraments become effectual means of salvation?

Answer: The sacraments become effectual means of salvation, not from any virtue in them, or in him that doth administer them,[1] but only by the blessing of Christ, and the working of his Spirit in them that by faith receive them.[2]

Question 92. What is a sacrament?

Answer: A sacrament is an holy ordinance instituted by Christ, wherein, by sensible signs, Christ, and the benefits of the new covenant, are represented,[3] sealed, and applied to believers.[4]

Question 93. Which are the sacraments of the New Testament?

Answer: The sacraments of the New Testament are, Baptism,[5] and the Lord's Supper.[6]

1. So then, neither is he that planteth any thing, neither he that watereth: but God that giveth increase (I Cor. 3:7).
2. The like figure whereunto even baptism doth also now save us, (not the putting away of the filth of the flesh, but the answer of a good conscience toward God,) by the resurrection of Jesus Christ (I Pet. 3:21).
3. For as often as ye eat this bread, and drink this cup, ye do shew the Lord's death till he come (I Cor. 11:26).
4. And he received the sign of circumcision, a seal of the righteousness of the faith which he had yet being uncircumcised (Rom. 4:11).
5. Go ye therefore, and teach all nations, baptizing them . . . (Matt. 28:19).
6. For I have received of the Lord that which also I delivered unto you, that the Lord Jesus the same night in which he was betrayed took bread . . . (I Cor. 11:23).

The Roman Catholic Church teaches that there are *seven* sacraments. These are: 1) baptism, 2) confirmation, 3) penance, 4) matrimony, 5) the mass, 6) ordination, and 7) extreme unction. The Churches of the Reformation rejected five of these (and went back to a more scriptural administration of the other two). They said that baptism and the Lord's supper, and these only, are really sacraments. Why did they come to this conclusion? They did so

96

for several reasons. We give them as they are stated by Dr. Hodge. First, in order to be a sacrament we must be able to show that Christ commanded it. Second, it must be a sign (that is, an outward and visible representation of an inward and invisible work of God's grace). Third, we must be able to show from Scripture that the ordinance is perpetual (that is, that Christ commanded His Church to observe it till He comes). Finally, it must be shown that the ordinance is a seal intended to confirm and strengthen the faith of those who receive it. Since baptism and communion (and these alone) meet these qualifications they are properly called sacraments. The other ceremonies and ordinances of the Roman Catholic Church are not really sacraments because they do not meet these scriptural qualifications.

A second major error of the Roman Catholic Church, as respects the sacraments, concerns the efficacy thereof. In order for a sacrament to work God's grace in the hearts of men, says Roman Catholic teaching, two things are necessary—first, the sacrament must be administered according to proper form—and second, it must be administered with the right intention. If the sacrament is administered in *the way* the Roman Catholic Church says it should be administered, and with *the intention* that this same Church prescribes, then there will be an operation of God. The power of God in all such cases, it is said, is contained within the sacrament itself. We reject this view of the sacraments for the following reasons. Only God can know the heart (Heb. 4:12). If the validity of the sacrament depended upon the inward spiritual condition (intention) of the minister, then, we would never be sure that we had received God's blessing. "Jesus knew from the beginning who should betray him," says the Bible (John 6:64). Yet "Jesus himself baptized not, but his disciples" (John 4:2). And one of the disciples was Judas. Yet never does our Lord suggest that there was anything invalid about this baptism. The warnings of Scripture to the effect that we must examine ourselves (I Cor. 11:20-30) plainly teach us that the benefit of the sacrament depends upon *our* intention, not the intention of the minister. It is important, of course, that the sacraments be rightly administered. The Church should follow the rule of Scripture as closely as possible. We can hardly expect God to bless the sacraments when they are not so administered. But this is no reason to forget that God is sovereign still—He works through these sacraments only as He will.

The sacraments, then, are *signs* and *seals*. To understand this is to understand the sacraments' essential nature. But what is a sign? It is, in simplest terms, a picture, or symbol. It is a visible representation of something we

Fig. A.

Fig. B.

DIPLOMA
Shorty Wescott

cannot see. We see this in the illustration given in Figure A. Here we have a road-side sign. It has on it a symbol (or picture) of something that a driver of a car cannot see because it lies over the hill. The picture informs the driver. By looking at this sign he gains a true conception of something (as yet) unseen. The sign is a true visible representation of a real, but invisible, situation. And it is much the same with the sacraments. The sacraments give us a picture of a work of God's grace. There is this difference, however: the sacraments are motion pictures (or action symbols). (We will go on in the next two lessons to show what baptism is a sign of, and what the Lord's Supper is a sign of. Here we merely emphasize the fact that the sacraments are signs.)

In Figure B we illlustrate the meaning of a seal. Here we have a high-school diploma. To it the official seal of the school is affixed. What does this mean? It means that Shorty's graduation (his successful completion of the required course of study) is genuine—it is attested and confirmed, in other words, by proper authority. If anyone doubts that he is a graduate, he only needs to show them this seal. And so it is with the sacraments. They certify the genuineness of the benefits that believers receive from Christ. (This is why a person eats and drinks judgment at the Lord's table if he does not believe. In such a case he uses an official seal when he has no right to use it!)

The Catechism speaks of the sacraments as "sensible." This does not mean that they make sense (to an *unconverted* person they may not make sense at all). The word here has a different meaning: it means that the sacraments impress the five senses—sight, hearing, feeling, taste, and smell. Since God made man a physical, as well as spiritual, being, He himself has given sacra-

98

ments that bring us spiritual blessings through physical means. In this way we receive the *same* gospel that is preached in a different form. The sacraments, as someone has said, are a kind of "visible sermon." They present the same truth, but in a varied way. It was for this reason that John Calvin, the great Reformer, argued against the use of pictures and images of the Lord. "It appears to me extremely unworthy," he said, "to receive any other images, than those natural and expressive ones which the Lord has consecrated in his word: I mean Baptism, and the Supper of the Lord" (*Inst.*, Book I, Ch. 11).

One final point needs to be made. The sacraments are not outward instruments only. In order for a sacrament to be a sacrament there must be a divinely instituted relationship between the outward instrument and the inward grace. As Figure A reminds us, a sign has meaning only because *it stands in relation to* what is over the hill! Likewise in the sacrament, the outward and sensible—by God's appointment—has a relationship with the inward and spiritual. The sacraments rightly administered, therefore, are never null and void. They always mean something. The person who comes to the Lord's table, for example, will obtain either blessing or judgment. If the sign is removed—taken out of relationship to the crossroad (Figure A)—then, of course, it does become null and void. It is no longer a *true* sign. This is what it would be like if a person tried to baptize himself, or observe the Lord's Supper privately and alone at home. A sacrament ceases to be a sacrament when it is separated from the Church—from the preached word and the congregation of God's people. But of this we shall learn more in our next two lessons!

Questions:

1. How many sacraments are there according to the Roman Catholic teaching? Name them.
2. How many sacraments are there in the Reformed view? Name them.
3. State two or three qualifications essential to a sacrament in the Reformed view.
4. What are the two things necessary for the working of sacramental grace in the Roman Catholic view? Prove this view incorrect.
5. What is meant by saying that sacraments are *signs*?
6. What is a *seal*?
7. What does the word *sensible* mean in the Catechism?
8. Why did Calvin object to the use of pictures and images of Christ?

9. Why is it impossible for a person to baptize himself, or partake of the Lord's supper alone?
10. How could this be illustrated with reference to Figure A?
11. Why is it not possible to receive a rightly administered sacrament without one of the two: blessing or judgment?

LESSON TWENTY-ONE

Question 94. What is baptism?

Answer: Baptism is a sacrament, wherein the washing with water in the name of the Father, and of the Son, and of the Holy Ghost,[1] doth signify and seal our ingrafting into Christ, and partaking of the benefits of the covenant of grace, and our engagement to be the Lord's.[2]

Question 95. To whom is baptism to be administered?

Answer: Baptism is not to be administered to any that are out of the visible church till they profess their faith in Christ, and obedience to him;[3] but the infants of such as are members of the visible church are to be baptized.[4]

1. Go ye therefore, and teach all nations, baptizing them in the name of the Father, and of the Son, and of the Holy Ghost (Matt. 28:19).
2. For as many of you as have been baptized into Christ have put on Christ (Gal. 3:27). Therefore we are buried with him by baptism into death; that like as Christ was raised up from the dead by the glory of the Father, even so we also should walk in newness of life (Rom. 6:4).
3. And as they went on their way, they came unto a certain water: and the eunuch said, see, here is water; what doth hinder me to be baptized? And Philip said, if thou believest with all thine heart, thou mayest. And he answered and said, I believe that Jesus Christ is the Son of God. (Acts 8:36).
4. For the promise is unto you and to your children, and to all that are afar off, even as many as the Lord our God shall call (Acts 2:39; see also Gen. 17:10; Col. 2:11,12; I Cor. 7:14).

Baptists insist that complete immersion (or submersion) of the body in water is essential to baptism. But the Catechism says that nothing more is required than this: a washing with water, whether it be a small amount of water (as in sprinkling or pouring) or a large amount of water (as in immersion). We can see that the Catechism is correct from the following facts. 1) There is not a single instance of baptism recorded in Scripture in which immersion can be *proved*. We do not say that it can be proved that immersion was never used. It may have been in some instances. But it may not have been. It cannot be proved in even one instance that it was. Thus we conclude that God does not command baptism by immersion. 2) There are instances in which it can be proved that baptism was not by immersion. We cite an example. In I Corinthians 10:2 Paul says the Israelites (in the time of Moses) "were all baptized." He says they "all passed through the sea" (v. 1). Yet we know from Exodus 14:22,28 that there was not one single Israelite who was immersed. Rather, it was the Egyptians who were immersed. Thus we have immersion which was not baptism (the Egyptians) and we have baptism which was not immersion (the Israelites). We therefore have proof that baptism need not be by immersion. 3) Finally we note that the baptism of the Holy Spirit (Acts 1:5,8; 2:17ff.) was by pouring. The Spirit was poured out upon the disciples. They were not immersed into the Spirit. This is very important because the baptism with water is compared with this baptism (Matt. 3:11). If the greater baptism is by pouring, then surely the lesser baptism can be by pouring also!

Baptists also insist that baptism is properly administered only to adults who make public profession of faith. There should be no baptism of infants, they say, because infants do not have the conversion experience of which baptism is a sign. What is our answer to this? Our answer is this: the central teaching of the Bible is the covenant of grace. This covenant is called the *everlasting* covenant (Gen. 17:7; Heb. 13:20). This means that there is *one* plan of salvation running through all history. There is also *one Church* (the people of God, who have believed God's promise) in all ages. The outward form has changed, but the covenant itself has not changed. The way in which the covenant has been administered has changed, but not the covenant itself. Let us illustrate:

ONE EVERLASTING COVENANT

THE OLD TESTAMENT FORM	THE NEW TESTAMENT FORM
Circumcision—Gen. 17:7 (1-14)	*Baptism*—Acts 2:39 (Gal. 3:29, etc.)
Administered once	Administered once
to believers and their children	to believers and their children
picturing cleansing from sin	picturing cleansing from sin
in a bloody type	in a bloodless antitype
Passover—Ex. 12:43 (12:3-17)	*Lord's Supper*—I Cor. 5:7 (11:23-34)
Administered often	Administered often
to adult believers	to adult believers
picturing nurture in faith	picturing nurture in faith
in a bloody type	in a bloodless antitype

God promised something to Abraham. He promised that Abraham would be the father of many nations. He promised that his descendant would be the savior of the world. And He promised to be a God to him and his children. This was an everlasting covenant (Gen. 17:7). The New Testament does not break this off to begin something new. In Galatians 3:16,17 we are expressly told that nothing can ever annul the covenant God made with Abraham. In fact, we ourselves (if we truly believe in Christ) are called Abraham's children (Gal. 3:29). From this we can see that there is no change in the covenant of grace except as to the form of administration. Because Christ has now died for our sins, we do not any longer need blood sacrifices or ceremonies. That is why baptism has replaced circumcision, and the Lord's Supper has replaced the passover. If we once grasp this great truth, we will be able to understand why there is no direct commandment to baptize infants in the New Testament. The reason is that there was no need to give a new command for something that God had already made clear. From the beginning God had included children with their believing parents. It was, from the beginning, God's will that children receive the sign and seal of the covenant along with their parents. Since there was no change in this fact (but only in the form of the sign and seal), there was no need for any specific commandment concerning the children being recipients. To the Baptists who say: "Show us where God ever put children in the Church," we say—it is recorded in Genesis 17. To the Baptists we therefore say: "Now please show us where God ever put the children of believers out!"

As might be expected, then, the evidence that children were baptized in the early New Testament Church is circumstantial. We will here give a mere sample of this kind of evidence. In I Corinthians 7:14 Paul says that children born to marriages in which at least one parent is a Christian are *holy*. The word translated holy is the standard word in the New Testament for professing adult Christians (often translated *saints*). Paul calls these infants *saints*. We therefore conclude that they were also baptized. Again, in Paul's Epistle to the Ephesians, the apostle begins his letter by saying that he is writing "to the saints which are at Ephesus" (Eph. 1:1). Yet in chapter 6 he speaks directly to the children (6:1-4). Thus we see that Paul regarded the children too as members of the Church.

But the most important thing to understand is the *meaning* of baptism. The Catechism speaks of it as a sign of our engrafting into Christ, and partaking of the benefits of the covenant of grace. This means that just as water washes away the outward filth of the human body, making it clean, so it be-

103

comes a fitting picture of an invisible work of cleansing and renewal. It testifies by means of symbol, just as the gospel testifies by means of words. And this means that baptism symbolizes the very same truth that we have already studied in earlier lessons on the Catechism questions. We have learned the *ordo salutis*—the order of the application of redemption. We have seen that man the sinner, completely dead in sin, is called, regenerated, converted (by repentance and faith), justified, adopted and sanctified (and finally glorified). And it is by certain of these "steps" that man is brought into vital union with Christ, and with God through Christ. It is by regeneration, conversion, justification, and adoption that we have union with Christ. And we notice that these "steps" in the *ordo salutis* are, like baptism, *once only* events. No one is regenerated twice. Nor is anyone converted, justified, or adopted twice. This is the same as to say that one is only once brought out of death into life, and out of Adam into Christ, etc. That is why baptism is but once to be administered to any person. It is to be administered only once because it is a sign (a visible representation) of something that takes place only once! Then too, baptism is a seal. It testifies and certifies the reality of *what God has done*. We emphasize these words because this is important. Some argue against infant baptism on the grounds that the children do not understand at the time what is happening. (This is true. Neither did Abraham's son Isaac understand what was happening when he was circumcised being eight days old.) But this, if anything, makes baptism more wonderful and sure in meaning. For it is a seal, not of man's ability, but of God's power and faithfulness. Thus when a covenant child is baptized he is not aware of what is taking place. But then, many years later, God may call that person to himself. He then regenerates that person by the power of His Spirit. He enables that person to repent and believe. He justifies and adopts that person. And, if that person at all understands what has now happened to him, he will understand that it is God who alone deserves the praise. He will say, in all humble honesty, God did it all and I did nothing! He will therefore look back on his infant baptism and say: "Yes, I see it now—I see that this sacrament truly tells the story of God's faithfulness and mercy—and it is a perfect picture of how He saves the helpless and hopeless by His own almighty power."

In conclusion we stress two points. First, the efficacy of baptism is not tied to the moment of its administration. The inward work of God's grace in a particular person may come before, or during, or after the time of administration of baptism. But the meaning is the same which ever way it may be. (Yes, this is even true in the case of a person who receives the outward sign and never receives the inward grace, like Esau of old.) Second, we must not think that baptism is of importance to us only once. No, the Larger Catechism rightly says that we ought to "improve our baptism" all through our life. Thus, whenever we see this ordinance administered in the Church, we are to apply its meaning again to our own hearts. Thus are we to deepen our understanding and thankfulness to God on account thereof.

Questions:

1. What do Baptists say that contradicts the teaching of the Catechism?
2. How would you prove that baptism need not be by immersion?
3. How would you prove that baptism ought to be given to infants?
4. What has not changed in God's everlasting covenant?
5. What has changed in God's everlasting covenant? Why?
6. Why does Paul say that Christians are circumcised (in Col. 2:11), and why does he say that Christ is our passover (in I Cor. 5:7)?
7. Why is there no direct command to baptize infants in the New Testament?
8. What kind of evidence is there that infants were baptized in the New Testament Church? Explain.
9. Of what is baptism a sign?
10. Why is baptism to be administered only once?
11. Of what is baptism a seal?
12. Why is it that *infant* baptism is quite as meaningful as adult baptism (if not more so)?
13. Can a person have the inward grace and the outward sign at the same instant?
13. What is meant by improving our baptism?

LESSON TWENTY-TWO

Question 96. What is the Lord's supper?

Answer:　　The Lord's supper is a sacrament, wherein, by giving and receiving bread and wine, according to Christ's appointment, his death is showed forth;[1] and the worthy receivers are, not after a corporal and carnal manner, but by faith, made partakers of his body and blood, with all his benefits, to their spiritual nourishment, and growth in grace.[2]

Question 97. What is required to the worthy receiving of the Lord's supper?

Answer:　　It is required of them that would worthily partake of the Lord's supper, that they examine themselves of their knowledge to discern the Lord's body,[3] of their faith to feed upon him,[4] of their repentance,[5] love,[6] and new obedience;[7] lest, coming unworthily, they eat and drink judgment to themselves.[8]

1. And he took bread, and gave thanks, and brake it, and gave unto them saying, This is my body, which is given for you: this do in remembrance of me. Likewise also the cup after supper, saying, This cup is the new testament in my blood, which is shed for you (Luke 22:19,20).
2. The cup of blessing which we bless, is it not the communion of the blood of Christ? The bread which we break, is it not the communion of the body of Christ? (I Cor. 10:16).
3. But let a man examine himself, and so let him eat . . . and drink . . . (I Cor. 11:28).
4. Examine yourselves, whether ye be in the faith (II Cor. 13:5).
5. If we would judge ourselves, we should not be judged (I Cor. 11:31).
6. Follow after charity (love) (I Cor. 14:1).
7. Therefore let us keep the feast . . . with the unleavened bread of sincerity and truth (I Cor. 5:8).
8. Wherefore, whosoever shall eat this bread, and drink this cup of the Lord, unworthily, shall be guilty of the body and blood of the Lord (I Cor. 11:27).

The Bible gives us four accounts of the institution of the Lord's Supper (Matt. 26:26-29; Mark 14:22-25; Luke 22:17-20; and I Cor. 11:23-26). In

106

these we see the simplicity and solemnity that ought to mark the celebration of this sacrament. Yet this very sacrament has been the focal point of some of the most obvious corruptions of the gospel. The statements of the Catechism are, in part, framed to warn us against these perversions.

In the first place, then, we note that the elements of the Lord's Supper are bread and wine. The body and blood of Christ are not present "after a corporal or carnal manner." There is no *physical* presence of the Lord. There is no miracle performed by the minister who distributes the elements to the people. The Roman Catholic Church teaches this error. It says that when the "miracle of the mass" takes place, the bread is actually changed *into* the physical body of Christ, and the wine *into* the blood of Christ. This is called *transubstantiation*. It means that there is (supposedly) a miraculous change of substance. In the Bible we have a real instance of transubstantiation. It is recorded in John 2:1-11. Jesus changed the water *into* wine. Before the miracle there was water only. After the miracle there was wine instead of water. And note that the miracle was self-attesting. Those who were there knew (without being told) that the water had become wine.

A. TRANSUBSTANTIATION

— CHANGED INTO →

water   wine

The Lutheran Church teaches the doctrine of *consubstantiation*. According to this view the bread remains bread, and the wine remains wine, in the administration of this sacrament. But, at a certain moment, the actual physical body and blood of Christ become present *in*, *with*, or *under* the bread and wine. This, it is said, is very much the same as when heat becomes present in an iron bar when it is placed in the fire. The iron bar is still there, but the heat now comes in and is also there.

B. CONSUBSTANTIATION

— ADDED UNTO →

iron bar   red-hot iron

According to either of these views (Roman Catholic or Lutheran), people are said to partake of the body and blood of Christ "after a corporal and carnal manner." That is, they actually are said to eat Christ's flesh and drink His blood as literally as a cannibal who devours the body of a victim. Against both these errors the Reformed view teaches that the bread and wine are all that are *physically* present. Only those who receive these signs and symbols in true faith also partake—spiritually—of the benefits of the one sacrifice of Christ. Thus Augustine once said that "Judas ate bread with the Lord, but did not eat the Lord with the bread." In this quaint way Augustine made a necessary distinction between the physical sign and seal, and the spiritual benefit which is received by faith. This is obviously the correct view. When the disciples first partook of this supper, Christ's body and blood were not changed—nor were they in the bread and wine—but were there in the person of Jesus Christ, who gave them the bread and wine. He gave them the bread, but not His own physical body, to eat. And He gave them the wine, but not His own blood (then yet in His veins), to drink. Thus, much later on, the apostle says "the *cup* of blessing which we bless, is it not the communion of the body of Christ? The *bread* which we break, is it not the communion of the body of Christ?" (I Cor. 10:16). "For as often as ye eat this *bread* and drink this *cup*, ye do show forth the Lord's death till he come" (I Cor. 11:26).

It is for this reason that the Catechism, following the teaching of Paul (I Cor. 11:28), devotes attention to the "worthy receiving of the Lord's Supper." *If* either of these (con- or tran-substantiation) were true, then we would have no need to examine ourselves in order to partake of the body and blood of Christ. But since we cannot *really* eat and drink of the body and blood of Christ except after a spiritual manner, self-examination *is* necessary. And it is in this sense that we understand what the Scripture means by eating and drinking *unworthily*. Some people have taken this to mean that a person *may not deserve* to come to the Lord's table. The truth is that no one deserves to come to the Lord's table. "For all have sinned and come short of the glory of God" (Rom. 3:23). To eat and drink in a worthy manner does not mean to do so as deserving of God's blessing. It means rather to have that frame of mind, and attitude of heart, which is fitting. And this means that those who are worthy partakers know themselves to be undeserving sinners, and such as have hope of acceptance in the sight of God only through the sacrifice of Jesus Christ. The Catechism speaks of "their knowledge to discern the Lord's body," which means that they understand the difference between the death of Jesus Christ and every other death. It means to appreciate the nature of Christ's work in suffering the wrath of God on behalf of His people. It means, in short, to recognize in the Savior's suffering and death the propitiation for our sins. So, the person who is *worthy* is really the person who realizes full well how unworthy he is and whose heart is therefore full of gratitude to God for the gift of His dear Son. "The sacrifices of God are a broken spirit: a broken and a contrite heart, O God, thou wilt not despise" (Ps. 51:17).

It is not enough, then, to recognize—or have knowledge of—what Christ has done for sinners. We must also look within our own hearts in order to see whether or not we have a right relationship with Him. We are commanded to examine ourselves in order to see if we have this broken and contrite heart— this faith in Christ as our substitute—and this love of gratitude which inclines our will to obedience (II Cor. 13:5). And here is where many find no little difficulty. It is not uncommon for people to feel that they have so little faith, repentance, love, and new obedience, that they are very doubtful about themselves. Let us be on our guard, then, against a wrong interpretation of what Scripture actually requires. We must indeed examine ourselves, and find repentance, faith, love, and obedience. But nowhere does the Bible say that we must find these things to be so strong and perfect that we can feel at all satisfied with ourselves! Even the great Apostle Paul, when he had looked within, could only say: "O wretched man that I am! who shall deliver me from the body of this death?" (Rom. 7:24). Evidently he too had only a small beginning of repentance, faith, and new obedience. Evidently he too felt himself to be a long way from what he should have been. Why then would Paul come to the Lord's table? Because he knew that Christ came to the world to save sinners. He knew that even though he was only a poor sinner, yet Christ alone was the hope and joy of his heart. Even though he had to bemoan the smallness of these evidences of God's grace in his own heart, in other words, he still knew that without Christ and the benefits of his finished work he was undone. In other words, it is not so much the *degree* to which these graces have developed, that we are to be chiefly concerned with, but the reality of them. It is the person who comes to the Lord's table without these thoughts who is really in danger. Such a one is like the Pharisee of old who entered the temple thinking well of himself. The publican who cried, "God be merciful to me, a sinner," is the man we should imitate (Luke 18:10-13).

If we come to the Lord's table feeling nothing so much as our need of forgiveness and cleansing—and the granting of God's strength to enable us to live more perfectly for the Lord—then we ought to come, and delight in receiving this sacrament. For here it is—when the bread is broken and the wine poured out—and freely distributed to those about the table—that we realize anew that our salvation is nothing more nor less than Christ and

His finished work. For "of him are ye in Christ Jesus, who of God is made unto us wisdom, and righteousness, and sanctification, and redemption" (I Cor. 1:30).

Questions:

1. What does *transubstantiation* mean? Who teaches this?
2. What does *consubstantiation* mean? Who teaches this?
3. What is the difference between the genuine transubstantiation recorded in John 2:1-11 and the fake claim of the Roman Catholic Church?
4. Prove from the first celebration of this sacrament that consubstantiation did not take place.
5. What would not be necessary if either of these views were correct?
6. What is not meant by the word *unworthy*?
7. What is it that makes a person *worthy* to partake of this sacrament?
8. How do we find out whether or not we are worthy?
9. Why is this often a serious problem for Christians?
10. What is the proper solution for this problem?
11. Who is the person who is in greatest danger in this sacrament?
12. How does the parable of the Pharisee and the publican help us to understand this problem?
13. What should our deepest thought or conviction be as we come to the Lord's table?

Question 98. What is prayer?

Answer:　　Prayer is an offering up of our desires unto God[1] for things agreeable to his will,[2] in the name of Christ,[3] with confession of our sins,[4] and thankful acknowledgement of his mercies.[5]

1. Trust in him at all times: ye people, pour out your heart before him (Ps. 62:8).
2. And he that searcheth the hearts knoweth what is the mind of the Spirit, because he maketh intercession for the saints according to the will of God (Rom. 8:27).
3. Whatsoever ye shall ask the Father in my name, he will give it you (John 16:23).
4. And I prayed unto the Lord my God, and made my confession (Dan. 9:4).
5. Be careful for nothing: but in everything by prayer and supplication with thanksgiving let your requests be made known unto God (Phil. 4:6).

Nothing shows the difference between true and false religion as does prayer. For in true religion alone is prayer "an offering up of our desires unto God . . . in the name of Christ."

The first thing we need to realize, then, is that true prayer—like true religion—is a matter of the heart! In some pagan religions prayer is a completely mechanical thing. Prayers are written on circular drums, and these are turned over and over again by some natural force (such as the water passing by in a stream). Each time the drum revolves God is supposed to consider that the prayer has been "repeated." And it is easy to see that such a prayer is hardly a matter of heart-felt desire. Yet even in many unfaithful Churches we find essentially the same thing. A good example is the Roman Catholic prayer called the rosary. Here the people pray the same words over and over again, keeping track of the number of times they have repeated themselves by counting the rosary beads. Here we are reminded of the words of our Lord Jesus Christ. He said, "When ye pray, use not vain repetitions, as the heathen do: for they think that they shall be heard for their much speaking" (Matt. 6:6). We see this same false tendency today in many

111

Protestant Churches too. Where false doctrine has come in, and the Bible is no longer accepted as the infallible Word of God, there is an increasing emphasis upon external things. And one of these externals is the use of written form prayers. The minister does not pray with and for the people out of the heart. He simply reads a prayer out of a book. Let us illustrate the difference.

In Figure A we see a large number of form letters. A certain senator has received perhaps 10,000 of these identical petitions. In Figure B we see a personal letter. Which will probably receive the attention of a good senator? The personal letter will, of course. This is because it costs nothing—and often means little—when a person simply signs a form letter, or petition, that some- one else has written. But when a person takes the time and pains to write a letter of his own, it does have meaning. This is not to say that no one who signs a form letter means something by it. But it is evident that our own words express our own true desires. And so it is in prayer. God is not interested in hearing nice-sounding prayers. He is interested in the desires of our hearts. The Bible says "we know not what we should pray for as we ought" (Rom. 8:26). Every Christian will testify that this is true. We have deep desires, but we stammer and stutter, as it were, when we try to express these desires in words. That is why "the Spirit itself maketh intercession for us with groanings which cannot be uttered" (Rom. 8:27). "He that searcheth the hearts knoweth what is the mind of the Spirit, because he maketh intercession for the saints according to the will of God." A true inward desire that is only felt as a groaning within is therefore a true prayer even though we cannot quite find the words to express it. But a high-sounding form of words that passes for a prayer in the sight of men may well be an abomination to the Lord.

The second thing we need to realize is that sincere desire alone is not enough.

112

The 450 prophets of Baal were sincere, no doubt, when they "cried aloud, and cut themselves after their manner with knives and lancets, till the blood gushed out upon them" (I Kings 18:29). But it was the brief, calm prayer of Elijah that brought down fire from heaven (I Kings 18:37,38). This is because Elijah alone prayed to the true God. And just as a mere form of prayer offered to the true God is without value, so a sincere prayer is without value when it is offered to any other than Him. It is for this reason that the so-called prayers of many religious people are not true prayers at all. A Roman Catholic will pray to the virgin Mary because he is taught by his Church that she will intercede with Christ on the sinner's behalf. No doubt it would be shocking to him to hear it said that this is wrong. Yet this is the truth. The very reason for Christ's coming to die on the cross was to open a new and living way for us It was to open the way for us to come to God. That is why Christ, in the prayer He taught His disciples, instructed them to pray directly to the Father. We will consider this teaching of our Lord in greater detail as we continue our study of the Lord's Prayer. But here we simply emphasize that it is not enough to have a deeply felt desire. It is also necessary to pray to the true God according to His will.

We will see, in the next few lessons, that the Lord's Prayer itself is a revelation of what it means to pray "for things agreeable to His will." But here we will illustrate one very important aspect of this matter: praying in the name of Christ. This does not mean—as is often thought—that every prayer must be concluded with a fixed form of words. It does not mean that we must always say "for Jesus' sake, Amen" at the end of every prayer. To pray in Jesus' name means that we come to God—and ask of God—in utter dependence upon the work of Jesus Christ. It means that we come to Him consciously on the basis of what Christ has done for us. This is the reason we may not participate in what might be called ecumenical prayer. This is a very common custom today. At public gatherings—such as the inauguration of a public official (mayor, congressman, president)—various religions will often join together in a prayer that "everyone can say." Thus, in order to please the people who do not recognize Jesus Christ as the only savior of men, the prayer will be offered in conscious avoidance of Him. In such prayer the consistent Christian cannot participate. But again let us emphasize that this is not a matter of the words only. A modernist Protestant—who does not really accept the teaching of the Bible at all—may offer a "prayer" that uses the words "for Jesus' sake, Amen." But it would be wrong to pray with such a person, knowing that he rejects the Christ of Scripture. It would be right,

113

on the other hand, to pray with a humble and sincere person who believes in Christ, and simply ends his prayer as Jesus ended the prayer he taught his disciples. The really important thing is whether or not the prayer is offered up to God out of faith in Jesus Christ. He is the way, and no one comes to the Father except by Him.

Finally, let us notice that the Catechism speaks of "confession of our sins, and thankful acknowledgment of [God's] mercies." This is essential to true prayer. And how very necessary it is to emphasize this today. For, as Prof. J. G. Vos has written, "there are multitudes of people who have only a vague, sentimental attachment to Jesus, thinking of him as a great teacher, a great leader, a great ideal of humanity, and the like. Such people are not really Christians, and their prayers, though they may mention Christ's name, are not really Christian prayers." Many today think of Jesus as a kind of aspect of the American way of life. Jesus is there to help us when we need Him, and so on. But there is no longer any experience of redemptive Christianity in such people. They do not know themselves to be hell-deserving, and miserable, sinners. They do not comprehend the meaning of the suffering and death of Jesus Christ as the one who was punished for the sins of God's elect people. And consequently they have none of this overwhelming sense of the wonder of God's mercy and grace that we find in the prayers of the Bible. But here again we simply see that true prayer is something that we just cannot "put on." It is not something we can fake, or manufacture. True prayer begins only when a man sees himself as guilty and wretched before God. We have the true picture in our Lord's parable of the Pharisee and the publican. The publican "standing afar off, would not lift up so much as his eyes unto heaven, but smote upon his breast, saying, God be merciful to me a sinner" (Luke 18:13). Jesus said "this man went down to his house justified, rather than the other: for every one that exalteth himself shall be abased; and he that humbleth himself shall be exalted" (Luke 18:14).

Here we see one good reason for leaving the discussion of prayer till last in the structure of the Catechism. It is only when the law has shown us that we are lost—and when the gospel has shown us how we may be saved—that we can go on to learn how to pray! Or rather, it is only after we have *experienced* the work of the law and of the gospel in our hearts that we will also be able to pray the way we ought! Prayer, then, is not something added on. It is not something artificial or mechanical. It is in very fact as necessary to the true Christian as breathing is to the natural man. For the wonderful experience of salvation from sin is only ours as we *begin* to pray.

114

O God, according to Thy grace be merciful to me;
In thine abounding love blot out all mine iniquity (Ps. 51:1).

Questions:

1. What is the chief difference between true prayer and false?
2. Is false prayer found only in pagan religion? Explain.
3. Explain how Figures A and B illustrate the difference between true prayer and false.
4. Is it possible to pray without saying words? Explain.
5. Is sincere desire sufficient to make prayer acceptable to God? Why?
6. Why is it sin to pray to Mary?
7. What does it mean to pray "in Jesus' name"?
8. Why is it wrong to participate in "ecumenical prayer"?
9. What element is mentioned in the Catechism definition of true prayer that must be emphasized today? Why need this be emphasized today?
10. Why is it wise to discuss the subject of prayer after the law and the gospel (as in the structure of the Shorter Catechism)?
11. In your own words try to express why there can be no prayer (such as the Catechism defines) without genuine Christian experience.
12. Be prepared to quote a biblical prayer (or psalm) to show that "confession of our sins, and thankful acknowledgment of [God's] mercies" is indeed emphasized in Scripture.

Question 99. What rule hath God given for our direction in prayer?
Answer: The whole word of God is of use to direct us in prayer;[1] but the special rule of direction is that form of prayer which Christ taught his disciples, commonly called the Lord's Prayer.[2]

1. And this is the confidence that we have in him, that if we ask any thing according to his will, he heareth us (I John 5:14).
2. After this manner therefore pray ye: Our Father . . ., etc. (Matt. 6:9).

When the disciples came to Jesus saying, "Lord, teach us to pray" (Luke 11:1), He gave them what is now called the Lord's Prayer. It ought rather to be called the disciples' prayer. He said "after this manner therefore pray ye" (Matt. 6:9). The meaning is that this was intended as a suggestive outline of prayer. Christ did not want His disciples to simply *repeat* these words. "When you pray," He said, "use not vain [empty] repetitions, as the heathen do" (Matt. 6:7). No, He wanted them to understand these words. He wanted them to see this prayer in much the same way that we would see a small model house. As the late Rev. Peter Eldersveld said, the purpose of a model house is not that we should try to live within the model house. It is only to help us to build a house that we can live in. And so it is with this model prayer. It is a pattern. We are to build our prayer life according to this pattern.

The first thing that we notice, then, is the basic concept of true prayer. It can be stated as follows: true prayer—like true religion itself—is God-centered. Just as the chief end of man in all of life is to glorify God and enjoy Him forever, so in prayer it is God who comes first, and only then our own interests. This will be clear from the diagram below.

Just as the ten commandments first instruct us in the worship of God, and then go on to teach us the life of service for God, so the Lord's Prayer begins with God. It concerns God himself then His kingdom, and will, before there is mention of our own needs. And yet do we not know from experience how directly opposite this is to our own natural impulses? It would seem that

116

The Lord's Prayer begins with God   and ends with God!

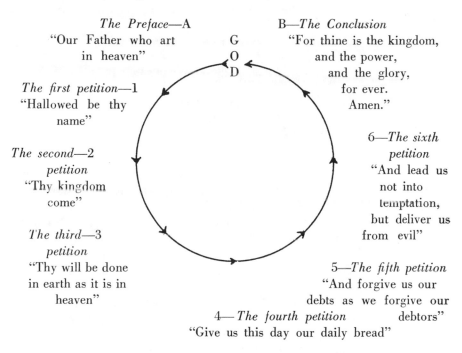

The Preface—A
"Our Father who art
in heaven"

G
O
D

B—*The Conclusion*
"For thine is the kingdom,
and the power,
and the glory,
for ever.
Amen."

The first petition—1
"Hallowed be thy
name"

The second—2
petition
"Thy kingdom
come"

The third—3
petition
"Thy will be done
in earth as it is in
heaven"

6—*The sixth
petition*
"And lead us
not into
temptation,
but deliver us
from evil"

5—*The fifth petition*
"And forgive us our
debts as we forgive our
debtors"

4—*The fourth petition*
"Give us this day our daily bread"

all men pray at certain times at least. In time of danger even professed atheists will cry out to God. But the natural impulse is to put self to the forefront, calling God in only in order that He might serve self-interest. So much false prayer is the very opposite of the pattern shown in the diagram. Even true believers *tend* (because they are still far from perfect) to go against this pattern. We therefore need to study this plan or pattern. We need to lay it up in our hearts. And when we pray we need to keep reminding ourselves to pray according to this pattern.

If this model prayer is *against* the natural impulse of our (yet sinful) nature, it will be evident that prayer is not easy. No doubt it was easy for Adam in his innocence in paradise. Surely he was then God-centered in his entire nature. To talk with God was then according to innate desire. But this is not true of fallen men. It is not even true of sinners who have been redeemed. They do more and more desire the things that are right. But while the spirit is willing the flesh is yet weak. There is a law of sin in our members warring

117

against these newly implanted spiritual desires. It is for this reason that we cannot accept the words of the well-known hymn as true to Scripture or to life:

> Sweet hour of prayer, sweet hour of prayer,
>   The joys I feel, the bliss I share
> Of those whose anxious spirits burn,
>   With strong desires for thy return.
>
> With such I hasten to the place,
>   Where God, my savior, shows his face,
> And gladly take my station there,
>   And wait for thee, sweet hour of prayer.

Much more true to life is the New Testament account of the disciples of our Lord, who were unable to remain awake to pray with Jesus for even one hour! (Matt. 26:36-46). If we study the Bible we find that even the Lord's faithful servants were often driven to pray by the circumstances, rather than by mere inner impulse. Think of Abraham praying for Lot in Sodom (Gen. 18:16-33). Or think of Moses praying that God would not destroy Israel (Ex. 32:31-35). Or Hannah praying for a son (I Sam. 1). This is not to suggest that it is *right* to pray only when we are driven to it. No, the Bible says that we should pray always, and pray without ceasing. But we do need to realize that there is much false teaching today on the subject of prayer. It is important for us to realize that prayer takes effort. It is not something that just becomes (as some have falsely said) as natural as breathing. The fact is that prayer—true prayer—like all other aspects of the genuine Christian life, requires intelligent and concentrated effort.

As we consider this pattern of true prayer, what are some of the characteristics that we immediately notice? (1) One is the utter *simplicity* of this prayer. There is nothing here of high sounding words, or poetic phrases. There is no use of words that have an impressive sound. The author once knew a fine Christian who had the habit of using this phrase in almost every prayer, "according to thy riches in glory through Christ Jesus." It is a fine-sounding phrase. But what does it mean? If we but listen to our own prayers as we speak them, we will notice this tendency to depart from direct and simple expressions. We will notice that we have a tendency to put a sort of "spiritual frosting" on the cake of prayer. This, we learn from this prayer our Lord taught His disciples, is quite unnecessary. It adds nothing. It only tends to falsify the true expression of the desires of the heart. (2) We also note how *brief* this prayer is. No petition has more than ten words. It is such that any

118

child can learn it, and understand it at least in essence. And yet how common it is—even among Bible-believing Christians—to talk about prayer as if it were the amount of prayer that matters, rather than the content. We forget that Christ himself said we are not heard because of how long we make our prayers (Matt. 6:7). The Catechism says that the whole Bible is of use to guide us in prayer. The pattern prayer taught by our Lord is a sort of summary of what the whole Bible teaches. And one of the things that we learn, as we study the effectual prayers of God's people in the Scriptures, is that they were never heard because of much speaking. (3) And yet, how *comprehensive* this prayer is. Instead of covering a little with much speaking, it covers much with little speaking. This is how we ought also to pray. God calls us to an intelligent interest in himself and all His works. He calls us, in other words, to a prayer life that embraces the whole realm of existence in heaven and earth. As we meditate upon this prayer, and think through the meaning of these petitions, we are amazed to discover that nothing is left out. We can add nothing to it, that is not already embraced within it. Just as we can work out our whole duty to God from the ten commandments, so we can work out our whole prayer-life from these petitions.

In conclusion we can say that this pattern of prayer lacks all those things that would tend to make prayer a performance before man! Jesus said this to His disciples just before He taught them this prayer: "When thou prayest, enter into thy closet, and when thou hast shut thy door, pray to thy Father which is in secret; and thy Father which seeth in secret shall reward thee openly" (Matt. 6:6). Prayer, then, is not something that can be performed—not true prayer. Whenever prayer becomes just a performance it tends to take on very different qualities, such as repetition, high-sounding phrases, and extended duration. True prayer, being an expression of a heart relationship to God, needs no such artificial aids. It is for this reason that we must not be discouraged when we find secret prayer hard to put into words. The false, popular conception of prayer is that we ought to find the words pouring out of our lips in a torrent as we seek God in the secret place. In actual fact, however, it is not like this at all. "For we know not what we should pray for as we ought" (Rom. 8:26), and often we find only "groanings which cannot be uttered" (Rom. 8:27). Yet *this*, rather than a false performance of going through the motions of praying, is what God delights to see. Just as a loving father will not despise or reject a request of his son when it is expressed in lisping speech, so the Father will not despise a sincere prayer because of its humble form. The deepest lesson of this pattern of prayer, then, is the fact

119

that true religion—and therefore true prayer—is *a thing of the heart*. This is why our Lord stripped away everything that could possibly obscure this fact.

Questions:

1. Why is the common title for this prayer somewhat inadequate?
2. What did Christ mean when He said: "after this manner therefore pray ye"?
3. What is the basic concept taught in this prayer? Where else do we learn this same basic concept?
4. In your own words summarize the thought presented in the diagram.
5. Is this concept against the natural tendency of the human heart? Explain.
6. What false idea is taught by the stanzas of the well-known hymn entitled "Sweet Hour of Prayer" quoted in the lesson?
7. Against this, what important principle to we need to keep before us?
8. What is meant by saying that the Lord's Prayer is characterized by *simplicity*? What is meant by saying it is *brief*? What is meant by saying it is *comprehensive*?
9. What are some of the charactistics that prayer tends to assume when it is performed for the benefit of men?
10. Why does Jesus stress secret prayer?
11. Is there something wrong with us when we find it hard to express ourselves in words in secret prayer? Why?
12. What is the chief thing to remember when we try to apply the lessons of this pattern of prayer to our own life?

Question 100. What doth the preface of the Lord's prayer teach us?

Answer: The preface of the Lord's prayer (which is, *Our Father which art in heaven*), teacheth us to draw near to God with all holy reverence and confidence,[1] as children to a father,[2] able and ready to help us;[3] and that we should pray with and for others.[4]

1. He will fulfill the desire of them that fear him; he also will hear their cry, and will save them (Ps. 145:19). In whom we have boldness and access with confidence (Eph. 3:12).
2. Ye have received the spirit of adoption, whereby we cry, Abba, Father (Rom. 8:15).
3. Unto him who is able to do exceeding abundantly above all that we ask or think (Eph. 3:20). How much more shall your Father which is in heaven give good things to them that ask him (Matt. 7:11).
4. Praying always with all prayer and supplication in the Spirit, and watching thereunto with all perseverance and supplication for all saints (Eph. 6:18).

We now come to the preface of the Lord's Prayer. It teaches us the necessity of a right relationship with God. We cannot really pray in a manner acceptable to God without this. And how very important it is to understand this today! This is because of the very popular—and very false—idea of the universal fatherhood of God and the universal brotherhood of man. This is the notion that God is a father to all people, and that all people are God's children. Thus it is common that people of entirely different religions will think it quite proper to "pray" together! Sometimes they will even repeat the words of the Lord's Prayer together. Yet the very meaning of the preface to this prayer is that no one can really pray to God acceptably until such a person is in a right relationship with God. In past lessons we have learned that we are not the children of God, by nature, but the children of Satan. It is only when we repent of our sin, and trust in Jesus Christ, that we are justified and adopted. Only when we are converted, in other words, do we *become* the children of God. Only *then* can we really pray this prayer. This is what our Lord meant when He said, "think not that I am come to send peace on earth: I came not to send peace, but a sword. For I am come to set a man

121

at variance against his father, and the daughter against her mother, and the daughter in law against her mother in law. And a man's foes shall be they of his own household" (Matt. 10:34-36). When we enter God's redeemed family in Christ, we leave the lost family of Adam. We understand—sad as it is to think about it—that even our own relatives who are not converted are outside God's family. *We* can say things that *they* cannot yet say. We can say that God is our Father.

But what does it mean to say *Our Father which art in heaven?* This we can best understand, perhaps, by way of contrast. 1) For it does not mean that God is so far from us that we cannot reach Him. This, be it observed, is a common feature of false religion. Take Islam (Mohammedanism) for example. According to this religion Allah is God who lives up in heaven. But heaven is so far away that Allah is not thought of as one who has compassion for men. People who live in Mohammedan countries do not have the same attitude toward human misery and suffering that we have in countries where Christianity is strong. People there tend to think that when trouble comes it is just "the way things have to be." They take, in other words, a fatalistic attitude. They say, "Allah has willed it." They make no effort to minister to the needs of others. And the reason is that Allah is so far from man that he cannot be reached by man. This same false notion also comes out, however, in corrupt forms of Christianity. Take, for example, the traditional teaching of the Roman Catholic Church. Instead of going right to God the Father himself in prayer, the Roman Catholic is taught to go to Mary or to one of the saints. The argument for this is that God will be more likely to hear our request if we make it indirectly, through someone who stands closer to God than we ourselves. In this conception, too, God tends to fade more and more into the distance. He is more and more thought of as one who is far away and difficult, if not impossible, for us to reach. The biblical Christian, on the other hand, knows that this is an utterly false conception. When a sinner comes to God through Jesus Christ (in repentance and faith) he is adopted into God's own family. He therefore becomes as close to the Father as any other child of God. He has as much right to come directly to the Father (because he believes in Christ) as any other saint of God. "Seeing then that we have a great high priest, that is passed into the heavens, Jesus the Son of God . . . let us therefore come boldly unto the throne of grace, that we may obtain mercy, and find grace to help in time of need" (Heb. 4:14,16). We are commanded, in other words, to come to God himself. For true prayer begins—not with some cry to a far off Allah—or a "hail Mary"—but with the wonderful words,

Our Father! 2) At the same time, however, it is equally important to remember that our Father is *in heaven*! And our right of immediate access to God does not in any way diminish the awe and reverence that we ought to feel as we come to Him! This too is very common today. For example, a Hollywood actress claimed that she was converted. She then began to speak of God in words such as these: "God is like a great big daddy. I could sit right down in his lap and put my arms around his neck and hug him, etc." Thus we hear God likened to a kindly old grandfather, or "the man upstairs." This false tendency to bring God down to the level of man is utterly unscriptural. For "to whom then will ye liken God," asks the prophet Isaiah, "or what likeness will ye compare unto him?" (Isa. 40:18). When Jesus told us to pray to our Father *in heaven* He wanted us to remember that God is still *God* even though He is our Father. God is, in other words, both near and far. He is close to us, and yet exceedingly high above us. He is our Father, but He is also in heaven. So, while we can come to Him—directly—we do need to take off our shoes, as it were, and stand in awe before Him.

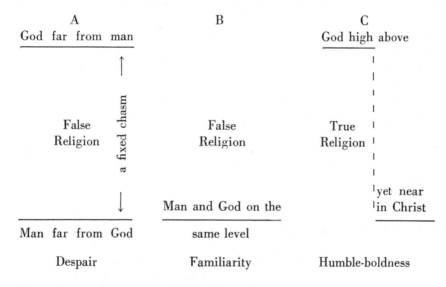

Here we see the way in which biblical Christianity avoids these two false extremes. It is not by a combination of these two false ideas. No, the way in which God is both high above us, and yet near us, is in Jesus Christ. Jesus Christ is God and man, in two distinct natures, and one Person. As God He

123

is therefore on a level with the Father, in His divine nature. As man, He is a partaker of our nature in all things except sin. As the God-man our Lord Jesus Christ brings us together with the Father without a false exalting of man, or a dishonoring of God. Thus we see why the believer can "draw near to God with all holy reverence and confidence." There is reverence because our Father is God. But there is confidence because God is our Father. There is reverence because God is in heaven, and we are on earth. But there is confidence because Jesus Christ has come to be our Savior. Through His saving work and present intercession we know that God is not only willing to help us (as our Father) but able to help us too (as the sovereign God of heaven). If He were only near, then we might despair that He would be able to help us. If He were only far, we might despair that He would be willing to hear and help us. But in Jesus Christ we have both of these aspects of truth united with perfect harmony.

In conclusion let us observe that prayer is ordinarily corporate: something that belongs to the whole body of believers, and not just to individuals. The Larger Catechism says we are "to pray for the whole Church of Christ upon earth; for magistrates and ministers; for ourselves, our brethren, yea, our enemies; and for all sorts of men living, or that shall live hereafter." As Matthew Henry says: "the two blind men did not each of them say for himself, 'Have mercey on me'; but both for one another, 'Have mercy on us.' " We all know how easy it is to pray only for self. And the Bible does tell us to pray individually. But here we see that praying together—and for one another— is an important principle of prayer. Our traditional mid-week prayer meeting is not necessarily the only scriptural way—certainly the day and time is not revealed in Scripture—but there is a biblical basis for coming together to pray *our* Father which art in heaven. It was certainly so in the Apostolic Church (Acts 2:42).

Questions:

1. What is essential *before* we can pray according to this preface?
2. What popular notion today contradicts this truth?
3. What important truth does Matthew 10:34-36 teach us?
4. What are the two false conceptions of man's relationship to God?
5. In what way are the prayers of Mohammedans and Roman Catholics similar?
6. Why is it that any Christian can pray directly to God?
7. Why must the Christian pray with reverence and awe?

8. Is the Christian view a combination of these two false views?
9. Explain how the great distance between God and man is overcome in Christ, without that great distance being reduced in any way.
10. Why is the Christian believer reverent towards God?
11. Why is the Christian believer confident?
12. What is meant by "corporate prayer"?
13. Is there a scriptural basis for the mid-week prayer meeting? Explain.

LESSON TWENTY-SIX

Question 101. What do we pray for in the first petition?

Answer: In the first petition (which is *Hallowed be thy name*), we pray that God would enable us and others to glorify him in all that whereby he maketh himself known;[1] and that he would dispose all things to his own glory.[2]

1. God be merciful unto us, and bless us: and cause his face to shine upon us. That thy way may be known upon earth, thy saving health among all nations. Let the people praise thee, O God: let all the people praise thee (Ps. 67:1-3).
2. For of him, and through him, and to him, are all things, to whom be glory for ever. Amen (Rom. 11:36).

Many parents have difficulty in naming their children. Books can be purchased containing long lists of names from which to choose. The difficulty is that names do not mean much today. One is as good as another (or as bad). So it is hard to decide which one to use. But it was not this way in biblical times. This is because of the fact that names were descriptive. The first man was called Adam (which means "man," or "mankind") because he was the one man from whom the rest of us come. His wife was called Eve (which means "life," or "life-giving") because she was the mother of all men. Names were statements of truth, in other words. That is also why names were often changed. When God chose Abram he re-named him Abraham (which means "father of a multitude") because God had destined him to be the father of the faithful. After Jacob wrestled with the Angel of the Lord he was re-named Israel (that is, "one who strives with God") because "as a prince" he had "power with God" (Gen. 32:28). In the Bible, then, a *name* is more than a mere label. It is a true description. It reveals something to us concerning the person to whom it is given. Thus the Catechism speaks of "that whereby [God] maketh himself known" as equivalent to His name! When the Psalmist says, "O Lord, our Lord, how excellent is thy name in all the earth" (Ps. 8:1), he means that these things that God has made are a true revelation of Him. God makes himself known to us through them. Of Him, says the Bible, "the

126

whole family in heaven and earth is named" (Eph. 3:15). This is the reason why God has many names in the Bible. He is, as Herman Bavinck has said, "a sun and a light, a fountain and a spring, a rock and a shelter, a sword and buckler, a lion and an eagle, a hero and a warrior, an artist and builder, a king and a judge, a husbandman and a shepherd, a man and a father" (*Our Reasonable Faith*, p. 133). And it is only as we learn to understand the whole revelation that God has given in nature and Scripture, that we understand His name!

Let us illustrate!

Shorty stands with silent respect before the great statue of Abraham Lincoln. Why is this so? There is a good reason. He has studied American history. He has learned much about this man. The name itself would have no meaning for a child who knew no history. But it has deep meaning for Shorty. And so it is with those who receive true knowledge of God "in all that whereby He maketh Himself known."

But what does it mean to *hallow* God's name? To this point we have been thinking of God's name from our point of view. We have been thinking of it as a revelation *to us*. Now we must think—or try to think—of what God's name means to Him. It will help if we remember the proverb: "A good name is rather to be chosen than great riches" (Prov. 22:1). Even a man should be more concerned for the honor of his name than for great wealth. Let us say a man has a reputation for being honest. He is then tempted to do something dishonest for the sake of money. He ought to say, "No, I would rather do anything than to ruin my good name." And however rare this may be among men, it is something like this—only much higher—when we think of God. For God *always* seeks to honor His own great name. When Jesus said, "Father, glorify thy name," the Father immediately answered, saying, "I have both glorified it, and will glorify it again" (John 12:28). God cannot deny himself (II Tim. 2:13).

When we pray this petition, then, we are not asking God to do something that He otherwise would not do. No, but we are—if we pray this petition with intelligence and sincerity—beginning to desire that which is dearest to Him. And it is here that we begin to see the radical difference between true prayer (prayer according to the pattern of this prayer of our Lord) and false. People will sometimes complain that they prayed and prayed and God did not answer. But what was central in that "prayer"? It was the desire that God would conform to the request expressed. What other reason could there be for saying that God did not answer? But what a difference it makes when a person learns to truly desire, above all else, the honor and glory of the Lord. When a person can say, "Lord, your honor comes first—and I want you to do whatever will bring honor to your name—and I ask only that which is to this end," what a difference it will make. This is one of the great principles that we see again and again in the great prayers of the Bible. Moses prays that God will not destroy Israel in the wilderness, for example, even though they deserved to be destroyed! But what is Moses' chief concern? It is not Israel, but God's honor (name) among the heathen nations (Ex. 32:11-13). If God should destroy Israel, he argues, then the Egyptians and others will think

128

wrongly of God. Again, Abraham prays for the city of Sodom. He is bold (Gen. 18:23-32). He asks again and again that God might spare the city for the sake of a few righteous in it. But what is the basis of this bold request? It is the conviction that God cannot do anything unjust. No, this would dishonor God's own name. So Abraham says, "shall not the judge of all the earth do right?" (v. 25).

It is here that we see what is so often wrong with our prayers. We pray for a great revival in the Church, for example, but we do not pray for the reformation of the things in the Church that dishonor God. But how can we ask God to bless the Church while it dishonors Him? Or again, we pray that God will bless our nation, or give peace, but we do not pray that our nation might be humbled and repentant to seek God's face. We pray for the things we want, in other words, instead of asking that which is to the honor of His name. Here we see why so much prayer is ineffective. It is ineffective because God *will* hallow his own name, despite what we may do. But imagine what a difference it would make in the Church—and nation—if people prayed with this first petition in their hearts. This is what made the Reformation period different. There had been many prayers offered by people in monasteries during the Middle Ages. People wanted revival. But when Luther, Calvin, and others began to put God's name above everything else (even the pope) showers of blessings came.

In our first lesson we saw that "man's chief end is to glorify God, and to enjoy him forever." The true Christian life is God-centered, in other words. We also learned that man (because of the fall) is self-centered. So a radical change is needed before self-centered man can become God-centered again. Here we see that this is true in prayer exactly as it is in other aspects of life. For this reason the Catechism stresses the fact that we are not, by nature, able or inclined to hallow God's great name. It is only when God enables us to hallow His name, that we can do so. Putting it in simple terms, then, the great problem is not to get God to do what we want Him to do. It is rather the great problem to bring the rebellious heart of man back to God as its chief end. David Brainerd, the missionary to American Indians in our early history as a nation, said: "My heaven is to please God, and to glorify him, and give all to him, and to be wholly devoted to his glory: that is the heaven I long for, that is my religion, and that is my happiness, and always was, I suppose, ever since I had any true religion; and all those that are of that religion shall meet me in heaven. I do not go to heaven to be advanced, but to give honour to God."

The man who prays this petition aright is one who has seen a vision of God in His rightful place. Having once seen this true God, there can henceforth be no rival to Him. "According as it is written, He that glorieth, let him glory in the Lord" (I Cor. 1:31). "Hallowed be thy name," he will say, fervently desiring that God would enable sinners to learn to honor Him, and dispose all things to His own glory.

Questions:

1. Why do names have more significance in the Bible than they often do today?
2. Why were names sometimes changed in Bible times?
3. Where do we learn God's name?
4. Why does God have so many names?
5. Why does Shorty respect the name Abraham Lincoln?
6. What does it mean to *hallow* God's name?
7. Why do we ask God to hallow His name if He will do it anyway?
8. What is the basic difference between true and false prayer, brought out by an understanding of this petition.
9. When God's name is our chief concern will our prayer be more, or less bold? Why?
10. Why are many pious-sounding prayers ineffective?
11. True prayer, like true Christian life, must be .... Is this possible with men? Explain.
12. What did David Brainerd desire most of all? What words of Brainerd show that he did not, in saying this, think highly of himself?
13. What must a person first have in order to pray this petition in his heart?

Question 102. What do we pray for in the second petition?

Answer: In the second petition (which is *Thy kingdom come*), we pray that Satan's kingdom may be destroyed,[1] and that the kingdom of grace may be advanced,[2] ourselves and others brought into it, and kept in it,[3] and that the kingdom of glory may be hastened.[4]

1. Let God arise, let his enemies be scattered: let them also that hate him flee before him (Ps. 68:1).
2. Yea, all kings shall fall down before him: all nations shall serve him (Ps. 72:11).
3. Finally, brethren, pray for us, that the word of the Lord may have free course, and be glorified, even as it is with you (II Thess. 3:1).
4. He which testifieth these things saith, Surely I come quickly. Amen. Even so, come, Lord Jesus (Rev. 22:20).

No one can really pray as God commands until he comes to know God as He is. Thus we have seen that true prayer begins with a vision of God. *Our Father which art in heaven*, we will say, *hallowed be thy name.* Sinful man, by nature, puts himself in the center. He sees everything else in relationship to self! He says, in effect, "let my name be honored, my kingdom come, and my will be done." But with the believer it is God who once again occupies the central place. Everything is seen in relationship to Him. And so, after expressing concern for God, above all (hallowed be thy name), he goes on to pray for the advancement of His kingdom, and the doing of His will!

But what does it mean to say *thy kingdom come?* What is the nature of this kingdom of God for which we pray? We begin by saying that it is (1) a *spiritual* kingdom. This is not the only word we could use, or even entirely satisfactory. But we do need some way to distinguish between the rule of God which does already exist, and that which does not yet exist as it will in the future. The Bible say God already rules over all things. "He doeth according to his will in the army of heaven, and among the inhabitants of the earth: and none can stay his hand, or say unto him, What doest thou?" (Dan. 4:35). Some have imagined that Satan stands outside of God's con-

131

trol. They think of the universe as having two ultimate powers (good and evil. God and Satan). But Scripture clearly teaches us that there is only one ultimate power. Satan exists, and he does seek to overthrow the King of heaven. But somehow (and we do not fully understand this) God rules over everything, including Satan. We see this quite clearly in the book of Job. "And the Lord said unto Satan, Behold, all that he [Job] hath is in thy power; only upon himself put not forth thine hand" (Job 1:12). Satan is allowed to do what he does. But God also says to him, "this far and no farther." When we say *thy kingdom come*, then, we are not praying that God will get control of all things. He already has this control. What we are praying for is what we sometimes call the kingdom of grace. We pray that the Spirit of God will work in the hearts of men to enable them to will and do that which is pleasing to God. We might say that all men *are* ruled by God "from the outside" by God's absolute sovereignty. But some men are also ruled "from the inside" (by God's Spirit) so that they are doing what God wants them to do because they want to. This is what we mean by God's spiritual kingdom.

There is another reason for calling this a spiritual kingdom. It is because some have imagined that we are to pray for a political kingdom. This was the tragic error of the Jews. They looked for a Messiah who would make their nation great. So today there are Christians who look for Jesus to return to the earth to set up what they call His millennial kingdom. They believe that He will come to rule here on earth, as an earthly king, sitting on a visible throne in Jerusalem for a thousand years. But what did Jesus say? "The kingdom of God cometh not with observation: neither shall they say, Lo, here, or Lo, there! for behold, the kingdom of God is within you" (Luke 17:20). "My kingdom is not of this world," he insisted (John 18:36). The kingdom for which we pray in this petition is not political. It has nothing to do with a particular city or nation. It is the rule of God in the hearts of his people. It is a kingdom that knows no national boundaries. It wins its victories by the Word and Spirit of God.

This brings us to notice that it is (2) an *antithetical* kingdom. This means that it stands in opposition to everything else. Paul the Apostle speaks of "the spirit that now worketh in the children of disobedience" (Eph. 2:2). Behind the various systems of thought—the various cultures—and movements among men, in other words, there is a higher power. It is Satan who is called the "god" of this world. When Satan brought about the fall of mankind he usurped this position. And the work of Jesus Christ is going to bring about his ulti-

132

mate overthrow. This means, as the Catechism says, that people have to be brought out of Satan's kingdom, and brought into Christ's. They must also be kept in Christ's kingdom. There must be a more and more complete separation from everything that is Satanic. But the great danger is that Satan seeks to deceive us. And this he does when we forget that Christ's kingdom is radically opposed to his at every point. We have an example of this deception in the sphere of education. For many years Christian people have imagined that there could be a *neutral* system of education. But Satan is not neutral, and neither are his servants. Thus we have seen one restriction after another placed upon Christians in what was supposed to be a neutral system of education. Christians should have realized that this would not work. *They should have been the ones who pressed the antithesis, by demanding an education for their children that is only and entirely Christian. This is what we mean when we pray this petition: we are praying for war—conflict—and victory, a world in which everything will be wholly on God's side.

But the kingdom of Christ is also antithetical in method. For, as Paul once wrote, "the weapons of our warfare are not carnal, but mighty through God to the pulling down of strongholds; casting down imaginations, and every high thing that exalteth itself against the knowledge of God" (II Cor. 10:4). This is one of the great lessons of Church history. Christianity conquered the Roman Empire without recourse to violent methods. Caesar persecuted Christians to the death. Christians replied with love and kindness. But then, centuries later, when the Church became powerful (and corrupt) it began to use the evil methods of the world. The great "Crusades" were an attempt to use the power of the sword to do the work that should have been done by the power of the word. But it only harmed the cause of Christ. True Christianity never says "the end justifies the means." It never says, "We can use the same evil methods the world uses, so long as our aim is noble." No, the method is antithetical quite as much as the goal.

Finally we note that it is (3) an *eschatological* kingdom. This term is the technical word for "last things." When we deal with eschatology we deal with the future; with the final issue of things. When the Catechism speaks of the kingdom of glory it simply means that God's kingdom will not come in the final and ultimate sense until Christ returns to restore all things. This is brought out clearly in Christ's parable of the wheat and the tares. Wherever the wheat is sown the enemy sows tares. The servants of God want to go and uproot these tares. But no, says the Lord, "lest while ye gather up the tares, ye root up also the wheat with them. Let both grow together until the harvest:

133

and in the time of harvest I will say to the reapers, gather together first the tares, and bind them in bundles to burn them; but gather the wheat into my barn" (Matt. 13:30). Since Jesus says "the harvest is the end of the world" (vs. 39), we may not expect a complete victory for the kingdom of God before the end of the age. It is for this reason that we must beware of all systems of Bible teaching that promise a golden age—or millennium—before the return of Christ, or the end of the age.

At the same time, however, we need to realize that the kingdom is even now in the process of coming! Often it seems that this is not the case. Christ's cause so often appears weak in the world. Yet how clearly the Bible speaks of the victory that Christ has already won (I John 5:4; I Cor. 15:54,55). God has promised Christ "the uttermost parts of the earth for [his] possession" (Ps. 2:8). "He shall not fail or be discouraged," says the prophet, "till he has set judgment in the earth" (Isa. 42:4). So one day there will be "the removing of those things that are shaken, as of things that are made, that those things which cannot be shaken may remain" (Heb. 12:27). Let us try to illustrate.

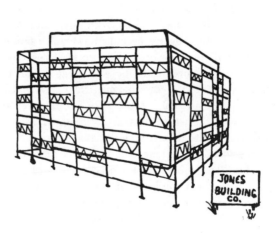

If we think of God's kingdom as a building it will be like this. Underneath the scaffolding of the old building (this present world) a new building is being erected. We do not see much of it yet. In fact, what we see often seems to deteriorate. The old seems to get worse while the new is being built. But God's kingdom is advancing. One day the Lord will come and shake the earth and the old will come tumbling down. All that will be left will be the new building (kingdom). Then we will understand better than we do now. Then we will be able to say, "the kingdoms of this world are become the kingdom of our Lord, and of his Christ; and he shall reign for ever and ever" (Rev. 11:15).

Questions:

1. What are the three characteristics of the kingdom for which we pray in this petition?
2. Briefly define each of these terms.
3. What is meant by God's absolute sovereignty?
4. How does the rule of God's kingdom differ from the rule of His sovereignty?
5. Prove that Christ's kingdom will not be earthly or political.
6. Why is it a mistake to blame all our problems today on the communists?
7. Why cannot education be neutral?
8. What were the Crusades? Why were they wrong?
9. What does the Catechism mean by "the kingdom of glory"?
10. When will the kingdom of glory be realized? Prove.
11. What truths does the illustration help you to see?
12. Can you understand this famous statement: "There are two kings and two kingdoms in Scotland"?

LESSON TWENTY-EIGHT

Question 103. What do we pray for in the third petition?

Answer: In the third petition (which is *Thy will be done in earth, as it is in heaven*), we pray that God, by his grace, would make us able and willing to know, obey,[1] and submit to his will in all things,[2] as the angels do in heaven.[3]

1. For it is God which worketh in you both to will and to do of his good pleasure (Phil. 2:3). Open thou mine eyes, that I may behold wondrous things out of thy law (Ps. 119:18).
2. Father, if this cup may not pass away from me, except I drink it, thy will be done (Matt. 26:42). The will of the Lord be done (Acts 21:14). The Lord gave, and the Lord hath taken away; blessed be the name of the Lord (Job 1:21).
3. Bless the Lord, ye his angels, that excel in strength, that do his commandments, hearkening unto the voice of his word (Ps. 103:20).

In order for God to be glorified there must be a kingdom over which He rules, and in which He is central. Thus we have seen that the second petition is a means to the fulfillment of the first. Here we further note that "the most important part of God's kingdom lies in His will being done" (Calvin). So the third petition is a means to the fulfillment of the second.

But what precisely is meant by *the will of God* in this third petition? In answer to this question we note that "the secret things belong unto the Lord our God, but [that] those things which are revealed belong unto us and to our children for ever, that we may do all the words of this law" (Deut. 29:29). So we have "the secret things" on the one hand, and "those things which are revealed" on the other. And we refer to both of these aspects of the will of God when we say "thy will be done." (1) The *secret* will of God (which is also called His decretive will) is simply the plan of God. The Bible tells us that God works all things after the counsel of His own will (Eph. 1:11). Thus a sparrow cannot fall to the ground except it be the will of God (Matt. 10:29). And everything that happens *is* a realization of the will (or plan) of God (Dan. 4:35). Now the important thing to understand concerning this secret will of God is this: we cannot know what this will of God is until we see what actually happens in the events of the world. Every time we read our daily paper, in other words, we are "catching up" (as it were) on our knowledge of this secret will of God. And there is no way that we can know before what this will of God will be. It is for this reason that the Bible strongly condemns such things as astrology (Isa. 47:13,14), fortune telling (Mic. 5:12), palm reading, and so on (Deut. 18:10-12). People want to know what is going to happen and so they try to pry into these secret things of God. But this is contrary to God's ordinance. (2) The *revealed* will of God is the only rule by which man is to walk. God has given to man, in His written word, a complete revelation of His will (II Tim. 3:16,17). It provides all that man needs, in any given situation, in order to know what he ought to do to please God. Thus it is that we are to go to the law and to the testimony (Isa. 8:20) to know the will of the Lord. When Jesus said "not every one that saith unto me Lord, Lord, shall enter into the kingdom of heaven, but he that doeth the will of my Father which is in heaven" (Matt. 7:21), He was referring to God's revealed will. For it is only those things which are revealed that belong to us so that we may do them (Deut. 29:29).

So we see two aspects to this third petition. On the one hand, we pray "that God, by his grace, would make us able and willing to know" and "obey" His revealed will. And then, on the other hand, we also pray that God would "make us able and willing" to "submit to his [secret] will in all things." Think of Job, for example. Suddenly he experiences terrible calamities (Job 1). His property is destroyed. His children are killed. He is stricken with disease. All these experiences were appointed by God, even though they were brought about by the instrumentality of Satan. Thus, when Job's wife—seeing all these sorrows—says to him: "curse God and die" (Job 2:9), he answers: "what? shall we receive good at the hand of God, and shall we not receive evil? In all this did not Job sin with his lips" (2:10). Here Job was saying "thy will be done." He was praying the prayer of humble submission to the decretive will of God. Or take, again, the example of Joseph. He was a servant in Potiphar's house. The wife of his master was an unfaithful woman. She "spake to Joseph day by day" trying to get him to commit adultery with her (Gen. 39:10). But Joseph knew this was not the will (command) of God. Therefore he ran away from her presence (39:12). He was saying, in effect, "thy will be done." He was saying that God's holy commandment alone is the proper rule for *our* actions.

While we may think of these two aspects of the will of God, then, and

137

keep them distinct in our minds, we must not separate them. We must not think that we ever have one of these aspects in isolation. Let us illustrate.

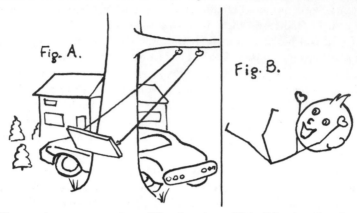

In Figure A we see a given life situation. This life situation is constantly changing. For Shorty, let us say, it involves a certain family. It involves a certain time in history. War may come and Shorty may be drafted, and so on. And all this unfolding situation is the will (decree) of God. And Shorty should pray that God will enable him to submit to this as the will of God. In Figure B we see Shorty being led by the precepts of God's Word. This revealed will (word) of God does not change. It remains fixed, perfect, and complete. And it is Shorty's duty to pray that God would entable him to obey these commandments. But what we need to realize is that neither of these two (Figure A or Figure B) exists in separation from the other. In real life, Shorty is *always* in a life-situation which is unique. It is not quite the same as any other life-situation that has ever existed for him or anyone else. And it is in this unique situation that the word of God (revealed will) comes with its demands. Thus the task will be to take the precepts of God's revealed will and apply them within the ever-changing context of existence.

It is here that we can see the error of some very popular ways of seeking to know the Lord's will. The writer once knew a minister who used what he called "Gideon's Fleece" in order to find out what God's will was. He would then invent a condition (such as: if it rains tonight, or doesn't rain tonight), and on the basis of how God met that condition he would claim that he knew God's will. The error here is that he was seeking to use the unfolding disclosure of God's secret will as a substitute for his revealed will of command. This is what people sometimes do when they are members of modernist and unbelieving churches. The writer once knew a minister who claimed that he was praying for some indication of God's will. What he wanted was some indication as to how things would eventually turn out. What he should have done was to obey what God has clearly revealed in the Bible (II Cor. 6:14-18). We are never to seek guidance *from* our life situation. We are to seek guidance only from the Bible *for* (or in) that situation.

It is just as important, however, to realize that we can go wrong if we do not constantly evaluate our life situation. Fifty years ago, it would have been quite unthinkable for a Christian to attend church services 25 miles from his home. This would, in that situation, have required so much hard work for man and beast as to be a virtual denial of the rest aspect of the Sabbath. How easy it would be, then, to develop a tradition to the effect that going to attend a church 25 miles away would be wrong. But of course the life-situation today is so very different. Now it requires far less effort to drive even 50 or 60 miles than it did then to drive a team of horses 5 or 6 miles. The divine commandment ("Remember the sabbath day, to keep it holy") remains exactly the same. But the context—or life-situation—in which it must be applied is not the same.

In both of the errors above we see essentially the same thing: we see the attempt to reduce the meaning of this petition to a simple mechanical thing. Just as it requires no effort to obey an omen (Gideon's Fleece), so it requires none to obey a dead tradition. But it does require effort—and much prayer—to function as image bearers under God. And this is our calling. We are not to be conformed to this age, but we are to be transformed by the renewing of our minds. We are to work with the great principles and precepts of God's Word. By the gracious work and power of the Holy Spirit, we are to think out the meaning and implication of God's revealed will in order that we might know what is good and acceptable and perfect (Rom. 12:1,2). It is only when we do this that we will become, more and more, like the angels in heaven. They are not robots. They do not obey God as mere programmed computers obey men. No, they obey God as intelligent beings who comprehend what the will of God is, and delight therein. Yet, of even greater importance is the example of our Lord! In the face of impending doom He prayed, "Father, if it be possible, let this cup pass from me: nevertheless not as I will, but as thou wilt" (Matt. 26:39, etc.). He prayed that, if it were possible, the situation might change. But if not, then He prayed that even in the darkest hour He might be able to *obey* His Father in all things. So are we to pray, "thy will be done in earth, as it is in heaven."

139

Questions:

1. The third petition is really a means to an end. What is that end?
2. What is meant by *the will of God*?
3. What are "the secret things" referred to in Deuteronomy 29:29?
4. What are "those things which are revealed" in this same scripture text?
5. What are we to pray with respect to "the secret things"?
6. What are we to pray with respect to "those things which are revealed"?
7. Are these two aspects of God's will separate?
8. Give a Scripture illustration of the truth suggested by Figure A.
9. Give a Scripture illustration of the truth suggested by Figure B.
10. What are some of the erroneous ways of seeking to know the Lord's will?
11. Do these erroneous methods of seeking to know God's will in effect separate life-situation and moral precept? Explain.
12. Why must these two always be kept in relation to each other?
13. Can you give examples of your own of errors in this matter?
14. What is the difference between a robot and an image-bearer?

LESSON TWENTY-NINE

Question 104. What do we pray for in the fourth petition?

Answer: In the fourth petition (which is *Give us this day our daily bread*), we pray that of God's free gift we may receive a competent portion of the good things of this life,[1] and enjoy his blessing with them.[2]

1. Remove far from me vanity and lies: give me neither poverty nor riches: feed me with food convenient for me (Prov. 30:8).
2. And let the beauty of the Lord our God be upon us: and establish thou the work of our hands upon us: yea, the work of our hands establish thou it (Ps. 90:17).

In the first three petitions we have seen the supremacy of God. Calvin once said that "true and substantial wisdom principally consists of two parts: the knowledge of God, and the knowledge of ourselves" (*Inst.*, Bk. I, Ch. 1). We must first get this great vision, or understanding, of the majesty and glory of God. Then we must begin to see ourselves as small and unworthy in God's sight—and yet the objects of His undeserved mercy! Once we grasp this twofold knowledge that Calvin referred to, we will understand why this fourth petition is "give us this day our daily bread." There have been some people who have reasoned as follows. "It is much more important to ask for forgiveness of sin, or deliverance from evil, than to ask for daily bread. Therefore the daily bread spoken of in this petition must be some kind of 'spiritual' bread, and not the ordinary bread that we eat. After all," they say, "didn't Jesus himself teach us to take no thought for what we shall eat or drink?"

Now in answer to this kind of thinking, we begin by saying *the whole of man's life is religious* or "spiritual." The idea that some departments of life are important to God, and directly related to God (and so, spiritual), while other departments are unimportant to God, and not directly related to Him (and so, unspiritual) is contrary to the Bible. "Whether therefore ye eat, or drink, or whatsoever ye do," says Paul, "do all to the glory of God" (I Cor. 10:31). We are to live the whole of life as unto the Lord. And we are to

141

understand that our daily bread (that is, even the food we eat each day) is a matter of deep religious importance.

We consider, then, some of the great principles suggested by this petition. And we begin by saying that (1) *we deserve nothing from God*, not even our daily bread. This is, of course, a principle that every Christian ought to understand. Do we not learn, as elementary truths of the gospel, that we are lost sinners by nature, deserving the eternal wrath and curse of God? Are we not taught that God saves us from damnation entirely by His grace (Eph. 2:8,9)? Yes, we know this. And yet, somehow we have a tendency to forget it. Somehow this truth fades out of our thinking all too easily. And we fail to realize how much we are influenced by the spirit and temper of the "times in which we live." Is not the social welfare concept all about us? Does it not teach us to say that man deserves a certain standard of living, even if he does nothing productive? Are there not, today, many millions of people on state welfare rolls? And do we not all tend to think that we have a fundamental right to such things as our daily bread (and much more besides)? Do we not even tend to believe that a person is entitled to certain minimum necessities of life, regardless of whether or not he is a good citizen or bad, or even willing to work or not? It is true, of course, that a person's civil rights are not the same as his rights before God. A person may have a certain *legal* right to something in the the state of Kansas, to which he has no *moral* right from God. But what we need to understand as Christians is that we are to realize—and recognize before God—that we *deserve* nothing except eternal damnation. Isn't that why Jacob once said, "I am not worthy of the least of all the mercies . . . which thou has showed unto thy servant" (Gen. 32:10)?

A second truth is (2) that *we are utterly dependent upon the Lord.* For in asking for our daily bread, we are recognizing the fact that it is God alone who can give us the things that we need. It is probable that the word translated as "daily bread" originally referred to the daily rations of a soldier. It would thus suggest the fact that our food is given to us a portion at a time, and day by day. It would remind us of the fact that we are in constant dependence upon God to supply us with our needs. And here again, the very mode of modern life tends to blunt our sensibility in this respect. In former generations, when more of our people lived in rural communities, there was a greater sense of direct dependence upon God. Men commonly prayed for rain, and a good crop, etc. They were conscious of God's control over the sources of life. But today we tend to think of *man's* power over these forces rather than of God. And we tend to seek the remedy—when there is any lack

142

of these things—in man (that is, government, or industry) rather than God. We need, in other words, to learn the lesson that Nebuchadnezzar learned. "Is not this great Babylon, that I have built for the house of the kingdom by the might of my power and for the honour of my majesty?" he said (Dan. 4:30). Because Nebuchadnezzar no longer felt dependent upon God, he was— that very day—driven out to live as a wild beast of the earth. Later, when he came to his right mind again, he realized that he was dependent upon God. And it is this that we ought to remember at all times, and make mention of in our prayers.

A third principle that we learn form this petition is (3) that *we ought to be thankful and content*. And here again it must be clearly understood that we must take our stand against the world in which we live. For what is more basic to "the American way of life" than the desire for more and more? What do we see in TV and magazine advertisements, if it is not the idea that we would surely be very happy if only we had this new car, or that new house or furniture, etc.? The "good life" is constantly presented as if it consisted of the abundance of the things that we possess. And we are influenced to think that the things that we have are old fashioned and out of date. Thus, in American life today, the "status symbol" is important. We tend to value persons in terms of the money they make, or the property they have. Yet we know that this is utterly contrary to the Bible. Our Lord himself said that a man's life does *not* consist in the abundance of things that he possesses (Luke 12:15). He told us to seek first the things of God, and that necessary things would then be added unto us (Matt. 6:33). And the command of the inspired apostle is that "having food and raiment, let us therewith be content" (I Tim. 6:8). When we learn to humble ourselves as we ought, and to ask God for even the lowliest and most common things that we need as undeserved gifts, we will begin to learn how to be thankful and content.

Perhaps we could illustrate the basic principles as shown on the next page. All false religion tends to be man-centered. It tends to make man the important thing, rather than God. Prayer therefore tends to become a means whereby man gets done what he wants done. Thus we may hear people boast of the fact that they prayed for a great sum of money and got it, or for a newer model car, etc. There is the feeling that whatever they want, they can get, because of the "power of prayer." So Figure A. Very different is the God-centered conception of Figure B. Here we see man in his proper place. This is the way a Reformed Christian ought to see himself. He ought to see himself as nothing (in himself). If all the nations are as a small speck (cf. Isa. 40:15)

143

Fig. A.

Fig. B.

"I will lift up mine eyes unto the hills, from whence cometh my help." (Ps. 121:1)

before God, then what is an individual? The Reformed Christian will also recognize that he is fallen, and hell-deserving. He will then lift up his eyes to the hills, and will humbly petition God for even his daily bread. And he will ask for what he needs in order that he might then serve God.

We conclude with a further word on the aspect of thanksgiving. For here again we so often lack a biblical perspective today. Because of a false kind of piety, there are some who profess to believe in Christ who cannot *enjoy* the things that God has given them. There is a sense of guilt in the very fact that an abundance of blessings belongs to them. And some seem to feel that the only way to holiness and spirituality is to renounce these things, and perhaps engage in such religious activities as prayer and meditation and fasting. But the Bible says, "behold, that which I have seen: it is good and comely for one to eat and to drink, and to enjoy the good of all his labour that he taketh under the sun all the days of his life, which God giveth him: for it is his portion. Every man also to whom God hath given riches and wealth, and hath given him power to eat thereof, and to take his portion and to rejoice in his labour; this is the gift of God. For he shall not much remember the days of his life; because God answereth him in the joy of his heart" (Eccles. 5:18-20). Is there anything more rare—or beautiful—than a family richly blessed of God with the good things of this life, who yet render such praise and thanks to God that you know at once that God himself is their portion, and not these things that they enjoy to His glory? Yes, blessed is that

144

man who—in the midst of an abundance of things—can yet know how to pray, "give us this day our daily bread."

Questions:

1. According to Calvin, of what two parts does true wisdom consist?
2. How will this help us to pray this petition?
3. What great principle is denied (in effect) by those who interpret this petition as referring to other than ordinary bread?
4. What are the three principles suggested by this petition?
5. How is the first principle undermined in modern American life?
6. How is the second principle undermined in modern American life?
7. How is the third principle undermined in modern American life?
8. What do we deserve from God?
9. What great lesson did Nebuchadnezzar learn?
10. What should be the ultimate ambition for a Christian (Matt. 6:33)?
11. What is the basic contrast brought out in the illustration?
12. What is prayer according to Figure A?
13. What is prayer according to Figure B?
14. Is it necessary for a man who is wealthy to feel guilty?
15. What is the "spiritual" attitude toward the things God gives us?

LESSON THIRTY

Question 105. What do we pray for in the fifth petition?

Answer: In the fifth petition (which is *And forgive us our debts, as we forgive our debtors*), we pray that God, for Christ's sake, would freely pardon all our sins;[1] which we are the rather encouraged to ask, because by his grace we are enabled from the heart to forgive others.[2]

1. In whom we have redemption through his blood, the forgiveness of sins, according to the riches of his grace (Eph. 1:7). Then Peter said unto them, Repent, and be baptized every one of you in the name of Jesus Christ for the remission of sins . . . (Acts 2:38).
2. For if ye forgive men their trespasses, your heavenly Father will also forgive you (Matt. 6:14; read Matt. 18:23-35).

We now come to what is probably the most often misinterpreted petition. And it is worthy of note that this is the petition that our Lord went on to explain when He had finished teaching His disciples this prayer. "For if ye forgive men their trespasses," He said, "your heavenly father will also forgive you: but if ye forgive not men their trespasses, neither will your Father forgive your trespasses" (Matt. 6:14,15).

Let us first observe, then, that we have a *debt* to pay. Some modern translations of the Bible obscure this fact, when they use such words as "shortcomings" or "trespasses" here. There is, in the concept of trespass, the idea of a fixed standard. And we speak of shortcomings too in terms of a standard or goal that we are required to meet. We cannot speak of such without some reference to an absolute standard, which—according to the Bible—is the holy law of God. Every deviation from this absolute standard—no matter how small it may seem to us—is a very serious thing. Just as a flaw in a diamond destroys the value of the whole diamond, so the Bible says that when we offend against the law of God at even one point we are guilty of all (James 2:10). But this is not all that we need to understand. No, we also need to understand that, for every single sin, there is a debt to pay! The Scripture says the wages of sin is death (Rom. 6:23). And this means that no one can violate the law of

146

God and just let the whole thing go. We cannot sin and then just say, "It will be all right. I will just forget about it." For someone must suffer the punishment that is due for every sin that is committed. It is therefore important to speak of our *debts*, since debts are *obligations that remain until payment is made.*

It is here that we see the unscriptural character of the popular idea of guilt. For the whole trend of our culture today is to speak of guilt as if it were a purely subjective thing. People have guilt *feelings.* And the whole modern approach to the problem of guilt is directed toward these feelings. Books are written on many subjects—for example, sex—with the express purpose of convincing people that they do not need to *feel* guilty. They are told that these guilt feelings are due to the moral concepts imposed upon them by their parents, or society. And the way to find peace is simply by getting rid of these false external standards that make them feel guilty. Even religious books express this view, when they teach that God is not a righteous judge who demands justice, but only a merciful God who is happy to forgive everybody. Thus it is reported that a modernist minister once said to a nominal member of the church, "Don't you know that God forgives sin?" And the church member replied, "Yes, of course, isn't that what God is for?" The one thing constantly ignored is the most important thing: the objective situation, our indebtedness to God. When we sin against the holy law of God we are guilty, and we do have a penalty to pay, whether we feel guilty or not. It is true, of course, that we may feel guilty when we really are not guilty of a violation of the law of God. If, as a child, I am taught that a certain thing is wrong, when the Bible does not say so, then my problem is a misinformed conscience! For "to him that esteemeth any thing to be unclean, to him it is unclean" (Rom. 14:14). "For whatsoever is not of faith is sin" (Rom. 14:23). It is a sin to go against conscience, even if the conscience is acting under a false scruple. But the all-important fact is that real guilt may exist even though the conscience may be untroubled. In other words, while it is always a sin to go against conscience (because God says it is), it *may* also be that the conscience is misguided. After all the *conscience* itself *is not the final standard.* The law of God is. And until the requirements of that law are met, no man is free from guilt even though he may feel free from guilt.

It is from this reality of guilt as an objective fact that we can begin to understand forgiveness in the scriptural sense. For this is indeed a radical thing, found only in true Christianity. Some years ago the author heard a prominent bishop of the Methodist Church. He said something like this: "I

147

can't accept a slaughter-house religion. If God would demand the punishment of his own Son, before he could forgive sinners—if he could look down and see Christ crucified and find satisfaction in it—then I would have to call that God a dirty bully." Yet the truth is that this *is* the very heart of the Christian faith. We can see this very clearly in the ceremonial worship of the Old Testament. Every year the Israelites celebrated the great day of atonement (Lev. 16:11-15; Heb. 9:7). None but the high-priest of Israel could enter into the holy of holies. Here the Lord manifested himself above the mercy seat. The mercy seat rested on the ark. In the ark was the law (the two tables of stone containing the ten commandments). When the animal had been killed, the blood taken by the high-priest into the holy of holies, and sprinkled on the

1. Holy of Holies
2. Dwelling-Place
a. Ark and Mercy Seat
b. Altar of Incense

c. Candlestick
d. Table of Shewbread
e. Laver
f. Altar of Burnt-Offering

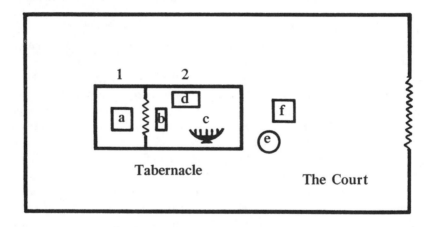

mercy seat, then there was forgiveness. And the important point to notice is that no one was ever allowed to come into this inner room except the high-priest. Thus the fundamental problem of sin was not "out there" in the court or around the court where the people were; but "in there" in the holy of holies *where God looked upon His holy law.* And the problem of sin had to be solved—not in them—but in the presence of God. It was only after the high-priest had settled things with God that he could go out and tell the people

148

that their sins were all forgiven. Only then could they have a basis for *feeling* free from guilt. It is only when the demands of a holy God are met in full that sin is really forgiven. And it is this that we have in mind when we pray "forgive us our debts." "For Christ is not entered into the holy places made with hands . . . but into heaven itself" (Heb. 9:24) "with better sacrifices than these" (9:23). "For by one offering he hath perfected for ever them that are sanctified" (10:14).

But what does it mean to ask God to forgive our debts *as we forgive our debtors?* Does this mean that our act of forgiving others precedes God's act of forgiving us? Or does it mean that we will only be forgiven in the measure and manner that we ourselves forgive? To ask such questions is to answer them. For we know only too well that we can only *learn* to forgive because we ourselves *are* forgiven (I John 4:19; Luke 7:47). And we know that nothing that we ever do is perfect enough to be an adequate standard for what God does (1 John 1:8). In our Lord's parable of the unforgiving servant we learn the correct interpretation of this second part of this petition (Matt. 18:23-35). A great debt is forgiven. The debtor goes free. Such a one ought to be thankful, saying "what a wonderful and marvelous thing to have my debt settled so that I am free." A man who has had this experience—and really understands what it means—can never be the same again. But read the parable for yourself and you will see what happened. Then you will understand what the Catechism means when it says that we "by grace" are "enabled from the heart to forgive others." The contrast will make it plain!

So our attitude toward others ought to reflect God's attitude toward us. We ought to forgive as we have been forgiven. And here too we see how radical the Christian faith really is. For when Peter came to our Lord and asked Him how many times he should forgive a brother who sinned against him, Jesus gave him an amazing answer. "Shall I forgive him seven times?" asked Peter. "No," said Jesus, "but 70 times 7" (Matt. 18:21 22). In other words our forgiveness of others should begin, in a small way, to reflect the boundless grace of God. We sin daily in thought, word, and deed. But even if we only sinned once each waking hour in thought, word, and deed, we would have well over a million sins to account for in one life-time. The Psalmist said, "Mine iniquities have taken hold upon me, so that I am not able to look up; they are more than the hairs of mine head: therefore my heart faileth me" (Ps. 40:12). To know the complete forgiveness of sin, then, is to realize that God's grace is beyond computation. And our forgiveness of others ought to manifest the fact that we are aware of this amazing fact.

149

Questions:

1. Is it better to translate the fifth petition with "trespasses" or with "debts"? Why?
2. What is the modern and popular conception of guilt?
3. Is it possible to feel guilty when God's law has not been violated? Explain.
4. Is it ever right to go against conscience? Why?
5. Is it safe to let our conscience be our guide? Why?
6. What basic truth of the Christian faith is offensive to the modernist?
7. In your own words explain how this truth is made clear through the tabernacle system.
8. What false interpretations are sometimes given to the second part of this fifth petition?
9. How can we be sure that these interpretations are not correct?
10. What did the unmerciful servant do after he himself had been forgiven? What does this prove?
11. In your own words express what the Psalmist meant in Psalm 40:12.
12. In plain modern speech express what Jesus meant when He said 70 times 7.

Question 106. What do we pray for in the sixth petition?

Answer:　　　In the sixth petition (which is *And lead us not into temptation, but deliver us from evil*), we pray that God would either keep us from being tempted to sin,[1] or support and deliver us when we are tempted.[2]

1. Watch and pray, that ye enter not into temptation (Matt. 26:41). Keep back thy servant also from presumptuous sins: let them not have dominion over me (Ps. 19:13).
2. Create in me a clean heart, O God: and renew a right spirit within me (Ps. 51:10). Restore unto me the joy of thy salvation: and uphold me with thy free spirit (Ps. 51:12).

The sixth petition of the Lord's Prayer confronts us with certain difficulties. For one thing, it seems to suggest the thought that God himself is the one who tempts us to sin. We say: "Lord, lead us not into temptation." Yet, the Bible clearly tells us that "God cannot be tempted with evil, neither tempteth he any man" (James 1:13). For another thing we say "deliver us from evil," which—in the original—can be translated *the evil*, or *the evil one*. And here the question is whether it is the evil one himself (Satan) or the realm or power of evil from which we are asking deliverance.

In order to understand this petition, then, we must first remember that *nothing happens to us in this world except by the sovereign will and determination of God.* "Whatsoever the Lord pleased, that did he in heaven, and in earth, in the seas, and all deep places" (Ps. 135:6). He "worketh all things after the counsel of his own will" (Eph. 1:11). So whatever temptation may befall us in this world can only be by God's appointment. It was no accident, in other words, when Job was tempted by Satan (Job 1, 2). Satan was granted permission to bring these trials and tribulations upon Job. Without this divine permission he could not act. Or again, it was no accident that David happened to be on the roof top of his palace when Bathsheba appeared (II Sam. 11:3). It was by divine appointment, just as it was by God's will that Peter "happened" to be recognized by the servant-girl (Mark 14:66-70). We clearly see, from such examples, that God does not tempt men in an evil sense: He does not entice them, or allure them to do evil. He does not "lead" them in *this* way, into temptation. But He does bring them into a situation in which Satan (and their own sinful inclination) can tempt them! For "every man is tempted, when he is drawn away of his own lust, and enticed" (James 1:14). This God never does.

But if this be the case, we may well ask, why does our Lord teach us to pray "lead us not into temptation"? It is because we may never take a light view of temptation. We may not say, "Oh well, if it is God's will for me to be tempted, then what can I do about it?" Neither may we trust in our own strength. We are not to imagine that we are immune to the power of the evil one. One reason for the many scriptural accounts of temptation and sin in the lives of great servants of God is to warn us against vain self-confidence. Professor Adams tells of a young man who passed by a certain movie theatre each day where sinful pictures were being shown. Each time he would resolve not to go in: and again and again he would succumb to temptation. When he was asked why he walked down that street to begin with, he saw the real problem. He had not wanted to avoid the temptation. But here our Lord teaches us that our constant prayer to God is that we might be kept from temptation. We realize, in other words, that we are weak and sinful, and that we are dealing with a superhuman power!

It makes little difference whether the *evil* referred to in this petition is thought of as a realm, or as a person. There cannot be a realm, or kingdom, without a king, and there cannot be a king without a kingdom. So *the evil* we pray to be delivered from in this petition can only be the ultimate power of Satan himself. And here we see an amazing thing! Within the absolute sovereignty of God (His absolute control of all things) there is a genuine place for the exercise of the power of evil. Truly, *this* is a great mystery. It is perhaps the deepest mystery that we can ponder. The greatest thinkers in the history of the Church have not been able to comprehend it. All we can do is to try, in some small way, to remember the greatness of God—for that is the ultimate solution to our problems—when we think about this mystery. In our illustration (next page) we see Shorty carrying a bowl full of water, with goldfish swimming in the water. Shorty has put them in that bowl of water. He can also carry them wherever he wishes. Yet within these limits, the fish are free to do as they "wish." They can swim or rest—eat or sleep—etc. They are able to do certain things freely, in other words, even though they are subject to a higher control that encompasses them. So it is with all God's crea-

152

tures, including Satan. Satan—despite his great power—is only a creature. He therefore exists within the limits that God has imposed. He can no more exceed those limits than can the goldfish exceed the limits placed upon it. Thus, though Satan may (as in the book of Job) use a storm, or a war, or an illness to tempt Job, he cannot wrest control of these things out of the sovereign hand of God! Thus, when Satan has done all that he can do, we can still say that God's control prevails. For, as Paul once said: "there has no temptation taken you but such as is common to man: but God is faithful, who will not suffer you to be tempted above that ye are able; but will with the temptation also make a way of escape, that ye may be able to bear it" (I Cor. 10:13).

It is such confidence in the sovereign God that enables us to pray the second part of this petition. We first ask that we might be spared temptation, because we are weak, and do not trust ourselves. But should it be the good will of God, for some wise purpose, to subject us to temptation, then our only confidence lies in the fact that God does work all things after the counsel of His will. And we therefore know that He can "make a way of escape." Here it will be evident that the same experience may be (1) a trial—a test—appointed by God for His glory and our ultimate good, and (2) a temptation in which Satan seeks to lead us astray. Sometimes the purpose of trial is to bring out the fact that there was no real love for Christ, and no real faith, in the first place (I John 2:19). Judas was tested so that it might become evident that he was not a true disciple of Jesus. Again, sometimes the purpose of a trial is to make a true servant of God realize how weak and sinful he is. Before Peter was tested (on the night that he denied the Lord) he boasted that he would never forsake Jesus, but would even be ready to die for Him (Matt. 26:33,34). Peter had to learn that this was vain self-confidence. The Lord also tests His servants in order to demonstrate His power over Satan. It was not Satan, but the Lord who won in the heart of Joseph (Gen. 39:12). In Job too, faith won over temptation. So God may have various good reasons for

153

bringing us into temptation. Yet the *only* motive that Satan has in using such occasions as a temptation is to destroy. "He was a murderer from the beginning" (John 8:44). And to this day he is our adversary who, "as a roaring lion, walketh about, seeking whom he may devour" (I Pet. 5:8).

Perhaps we can see the meaning of this petition best if we remember that our Lord himself lived so much in the attitude of it. While Peter—who had boasted of his courage in time of trial—was sleeping, Christ was praying. "What," He said to Peter and the others, "could ye not watch with me one hour? Watch and pray, that ye enter not into temptation: the spirit indeed is willing, but the flesh is weak" (Matt. 26:40,41). If there was one man who might think he had no need of prayer against temptation, it would certainly be Christ the divine Son of God, and the one sinless man since Adam's fall. Yet we see Christ praying that if possible this cup (i.e., this trial) might pass from Him. He did not boast. He was praying with tears and crying. And for this reason He was able—when He saw that this cup was not to pass from Him—to overcome the evil one. Our Lord, in plain words, did not fail in His testing, because He did not fail in His praying. *But this is where we so often fail.* James says we have not because was ask not (James 4:2). Either that, or we ask, and receive not, because we ask amiss, that we may consume it upon our lusts (James 4:3). Someone has well said that the battle is already half won if we really pray this petition with earnest sincerity of heart. The battle is half won, if I really *want* to avoid temptation and overcome Satan enough to sincerely ask it of God.

This petition, then, is for weak sinners—who do not trust themselves—who want to win the victory that overcomes the world.

Questions:

1. What are two of the difficulties in the sixth petition?
2. Are there "accidents" in our life experience? Explain.
3. How does God lead us into temptation?
4. If God does lead us into temptation why should we pray that He not do so?
5. What does the word *evil* refer to in this petition?
6. What is perhaps the greatest mystery in the Christian faith?
7. What truth does the picture attempt to illustrate?
8. To what comforting truth does this lead us?
9. What two things can a single experience be?
10. What reasons may God have for bringing us to temptation?

11. What reason does Satan have for tempting us?
12. What does Christ show us with regard to this petition?
13. What is the reason why we so often fail to win over temptation?
14. Why is the battle half won if we really pray this petition?

LESSON THIRTY-TWO

Question 107. What doth the conclusion of the Lord's Prayer teach us?

Answer: The conclusion of the Lord's Prayer (which is *For thine is the kingdom, and the power, and the glory, for ever. Amen*), teacheth us to take our encouragement in prayer from God only,[1] and in our prayers to praise him, ascribing kingdom, power, and glory to him;[2] and in testimony of our desire and assurance to be heard, we say, Amen.[3]

1. We do not present our supplications before thee for our righteousness, but for thy great mercies. O Lord, hear: O Lord, forgive: O Lord, hearken and do: defer not, for thine own sake, O my God (Dan. 9:18,19).
2. Thine, O Lord, the greatness, and the power, and the glory, and the victory, and the majesty: for all that is in the heaven and in the earth is thine. (I Chron. 29:11). Now therefore, our God, we thank thee, and praise thy glorious name (I Chron. 29:13).
3. Amen. Even so, come, Lord Jesus (Rev. 22:20).

We now come to the final lesson in our study of the Catechism. And it is fitting that we return, as it were, to our starting point. "Man's chief end is to glorify God, and to enjoy him forever," we learned, in the beginning of our study. Here we learn that as all things begin in God, so they end in Him. "For of him, and through him, and to him, are all things: to whom be glory for ever. Amen" (Rom. 11:36). Since our Reformed faith is—above all—the God-centered religion, it is good that we return to this thought.

Before we further think about this point, however, it is necessary to mention a textual problem. For it happens that the concluding words of the Lord's Prayer, as we find them here (i.e., "For thine is the kingdom, and the power, and the glory, for ever, Amen") are not found in many ancient manuscripts of the Bible. Many manuscripts omit these words entirely. Other manuscripts have words similar to these. And a rather small minority have the words as we find them here in the Shorter Catechism. It is for this reason that Bible versions omit the words, or place them in the margin. Since our ultimate standard of truth is the Bible in the original languages (Hebrew and Greek),

156

we must not accept anything as authentic that does not have the support of "many witnesses" among these ancient manuscripts. It is for this reason that we do not regard these words as an original part of the Gospel according to Matthew. At the same time, let it be clearly stated that we should have no hesitation in retaining these words in our Catechism, and in our use of the Lord's Prayer. This we say for one important reason: *these words express a truth that is perfectly scriptural.* They express a truth that we often find, in similar words, in the Bible itself. It is probably for this reason that, from a very early time in Church history, these words were used with the Lord's Prayer (as we find it in some Greek manuscripts). Christians, using this form of words in prayer, felt it appropriate to conclude with this simple ascription of praise and honor to the Lord.

Apart from the propriety of these words as a conclusion to the Lord's Prayer, they are certainly a fitting conclusion to our study of these principles of the Reformed faith. For the one all-encompassing principle of Calvinism is the supremacy of God. It is from this fountainhead that all other truths ultimately derive. (1) We see this, for example, in our view of God's relation to the world. For we not only believe that God created all things, by the word of His power, in six brief days, but we also believe that even now He controls all His creatures and all their actions. There are no accidents. There are no loose ends, as it were, and no independent agencies outside His control. For He does His will in the armies of heaven and among the inhabitants of the earth. (2) So it is in the whole sphere of God's saving work. The doctrines of Calvinism—man's *total depravity* and consequent inability—the eternal and *unconditional election* of the Father—the particular, or definite, or *limited atonement* of Jesus Christ our Lord—the efficacious or *irresistible grace* of the Holy Spirit—and the preservation and *perseverance of the saints*—all these are but varied ways of acknowledging the supremacy of God! They are nothing but an expression of the fact that God alone is our savior and not we ourselves! (3) And so it is in the realm of worship and service. When we say "the acceptable way of worshipping the true God is instituted by Himself, and so limited by His own revealed will, that He may not be worshipped according to the imaginations and devices of men" we are merely insisting upon the supremacy of God in the sphere of worship. And when we say that "God alone is Lord of the conscience, and hath left it free from the doctrines and commandments of men" we are upholding this same supremacy of God in the sphere of daily life and service! (4) Yes, we could even say that the Reformed view of church government is but an application of this principle.

157

To say "the Lord Jesus" is "King and head of His Church" is just another way of saying that the supremacy belongs to Him *in government*, just as it does in doctrine and worship.

It is true, of course, that all Bible-believing Christians want to honor the supremacy of God. That is why we often notice an interesting thing when men pray to God. Let us take as an example the famous evangelist, Billy Graham. Now Rev. Graham, in his writing, often denies the supremacy of God. That is, he often speaks of the will of man as supreme, rather than the will of God. This can be seen in his book entitled *Peace With God*. Here Rev. Graham places man's own act of repentance and faith prior to God's act of regeneration. Rev. Graham says, in effect, that God's act is dependent upon our will. And, in this view, man has the power to determine what God will do. But the interesting thing is that when Rev. Graham prays he very often shows that down deep in his heart he realizes this supremacy of God.

This is the point of the illustration above. For whenever a true believer is on his knees in prayer, this realization of the supremacy of God somehow seems to "break through" the false habits of thought, and even the false doctrines, that this person may suffer under. Thus it is common that a man who professes Arminian doctrine (as Rev. Graham: making man's free will a power that determines what God can do), will contradict that profession in prayer. Such a person will often ask God to change another person's heart so that that person will then be able to repent and believe. Furthermore, such

158

a person will often thank God for the fact that a certain person has been converted. He will thank *God*, even though—according to his own professed Arminian theology—it would rather be the man himself who should be congratulated for letting God do what He has done. Let us finally say that many people who are professed Arminians may yet, in their hearts, and in their prayers, put Reformed Christians to shame! As someone said, long ago, "better a warm-hearted Arminian, than a cold-hearted Calvinist."

What then is the aim that ought to characterize the truly Reformed Christian? It is simply this: to maintain in all the varied activities of life the attitude of prayer! Instead of *praying* out of a deep-felt awareness of God's greatness, and our own complete dependence upon Him, and then getting up to live as if this were not true—or only half true, we ought to rise up to live as if it is true (because it is). As someone has well said: "The central fact of Calvinism is the vision of God. Its determining principle is zeal for the Divine honour. What it sets itself to do is to render to God His rights in every sphere of life-activity. In this it begins, and centres, and ends."

The paradox is this: it is only when we grasp this concept—this truth—of the supremacy of God, that we also begin to know that joy and peace that passes all understanding. The Catechism speaks of the fact that we should "take our encouragement in prayer from God only." We can only add, yes, and we should take our encouragement in all of life's activities from this same wonderful truth. And just as we "in our prayers . . . praise him, ascribing kingdom, power, and glory to him" so we must learn to do the same in everything. We must learn to do this in every area of life—whether it be education, or politics, or business, etc. Or to put it another way: we cannot afford to be Christian in only certain areas of our thinking—such as in the personal and individual, as over against the corporate and collective (that is, in culture and society). This has been the great weakness in Christians for far too long. Vast areas of modern life and culture have slowly but surely become "secularized." Christ and the Word of God have been excluded. And what is needed now, more than ever before, is to return to the basic insights of this great Catechism—and begin vigorously applying them to everything in life.

As we rise from our study of the Lord's Prayer, then, it is good to remember that there is no area of life in which the attitude of prayer is not appropriate. The compartmentalized life is not the Christian life. The Christian life is—or certainly ought to be—one integrated system. For the simple truth is that all of life is religious.

159

With God alone my glory is
    And my salvation sure;
My rock of strength is found in God,
    My refuge most secure.

For God hath spoken once, yea, twice,
    And unto me made known,
That power belongeth unto God,
    And unto Him alone.

(Psalm 62:7,11)

Questions:

1. Why is it appropriate that we conclude our study with these final words of the Lord's Prayer?
2. Are these words a part of the Bible? Explain.
3. Why should we retain these words?
4. What is the most basic principle of the Reformed faith?
5. What are some of the truths that flow from this?
6. Can you think of another truth of the Reformed faith that flows from this principle which is not mentioned in the lesson?
7. Do Calvinists alone seek to maintain this principle? Explain.
8. What does the illustration show?
9. How will a consistent Reformed Christian differ from many other Christians?
10. Does a consistent application of this guiding principle of the Reformed faith deprive one of joy? Why?
11. What has been the great weakness in much Christianity?
12. What should be the goal of the Reformed Christian as over against this?
13. What is the main thought of these concluding verses quoted from Psalm 62?

APPENDIX ONE

Thou shalt not have more gods than me
    Before no image bow the knee
Take not the name of God in vain
    Nor dare the Sabbath to profane

Give both thy parents honor due
    Take heed that you no murder do
Abstain from thoughts and words unclean
    Nor steal though thou art poor and mean
Nor make a willful lie nor love it
    What is they neighbor's do not covet

160

WHAT IS REQUIRED?	THE TEN COMMANDMENTS	WHAT IS FORBIDDEN?
— to know — to acknowledge — to worship the true God	1 — The *Object* of Worship "Thou shalt not have more gods than me"	— to deny — to fail to worship Him — or to worship a false God
— worshipping as God commands	2 — The *Manner* of Worship "before no image bow the knee"	— worshipping by images — or any other way not commanded in scripture
— using God's name — and ordinances in a reverent way	3 — The *Attitude* of Worship "take not the name of God in vain"	— using God's name or — ordinances profanely (irreverently)
— diligent work 6 days — rest and worship on the Lord's Day	4 — The *Time* of Worship and Work "nor dare the Sabbath to profane"	— lazy or careless work during six days — superstitious observance of man-made holy days
— to honor — to obey God-given authority (parents, teachers, etc.)	5 — The rule of *Authority* "give both thy parents honor due"	— to dishonor — to disobey God-given authority (rulers, police, etc.).
— to preserve life for self for others	6 — The rule of *Life* "take heed that you no murder do"	— take our own life — or the life of others unjustly
— to preserve our own and our neighbor's chastity	7 — The rule of *Sex* "abstain from words and deeds unclean"	— to commit adultery in thought, word, or deed
— to further our own wealth or possessions — and that of others lawfully	8 — The rule of *Property* "nor steal though thou art poor and mean"	— to do anything that harms our wealth — or that of others
— to promote truth — and our own good name and that of another	9 — The rule of *Speech* "nor make a willfull lie nor love it"	— to injure the cause of truth — or anyone's good name
— to be content — to desire good for others	10 — The rule of *Desire* "what is thy neighbor's do not covet"	— envy; discontent — wishing evil to others

161